INTERNET JOB SEARCH

ALMANAC, 6TH EDITION

Adams Media Corporation
AVON, MASSACHUSETTS

Published by Adams Media Corporation
57 Littlefield Street, Avon, MA 02322. U.S.A.
www.adamsmedia.com

ISBN: 1-58062-787-0
ISSN: 1099-016X
Printed in Canada.

J I H G F E D C B A

Product or brand names used in this book may be trademarks or registered
trademarks. Any use of these names does not convey endorsement by or other
affiliation with the name holder.

Adams Media Corporation, a publisher of career books and software
products, owns CareerCity.com, a career-related site on the World Wide Web.
While the publisher is a potential competitor with many of the services and
products listed in this book, every effort has been made to ensure editorial
objectivity and impartiality.

Every effort has been made to ensure that all material in this book is
current as of the time of this writing. However, due to the nature of the
technologies discussed here, this information is subject to change. Readers should
check with the individual services and products to find up-to-date information,
such as current prices, fees, and features.

This publication is designed to provide accurate and authoritative information with
regard to the subject matter covered. It is sold with the understanding that the
publisher is not engaged in rendering legal, accounting, or other professional advice. If
legal advice or other expert assistance is required, the services of a qualified
professional person should be sought.

— From a *Declaration of Principles* jointly adopted by a Committee of the
American Bar Association and a Committee of Publishers and Associations.

This book is available at quantity discounts for bulk purchases.
For more information, call 1-800-872-5627.

Visit our exciting Web site at adamsmedia.com

Top career publications from Adams Media Corporation

CONTENTS

6. Researching Companies Online 241

The best places to find company information online, including where to find business databases on the World Wide Web and how to locate a company's home page.

7. Usenet Newsgroups 251

Discover the world of newsgroups, and find out how they can help you in your job search.

8. Networking Online 267

Discover the importance of "netiquette," and how making contacts online should be part of your job search strategy.

9. Computerized Interviews and Assessment Tests ... 279

Learn why you might meet with a computer at your next job interview, and what the computer tells the company about you. Information on skills, personality, and integrity tests.

JOB HUNTING IN THE INFORMATION AGE

Looking for a new job can be a frustrating endeavor, especially during times of economic uncertainty and growing unemployment. Competition for employment is fierce, as millions of qualified and eager contenders flood the job market. A single help-wanted advertisement in the Sunday newspaper often yields hundreds of resumes from suitable applicants.

At the same time, new electronic technologies are changing our methods of communication—and job hunting is no exception. Employers are embracing electronic technologies as a means of recruiting and attracting the most suitable job candidates. For instance, a job opening posted on the Internet can receive a response within minutes, and from interested job seekers around the globe. This means the applicant pool expands significantly.

Yet, regardless of their occupation or level of experience, all job hunters are looking for answers to the same questions: How do I get ahead of the competition? Where can I find that winning edge that will land me a new job? Today, those answers often lie with technology. Like the employer who posts job openings on the Internet to find the right candidate, the job seeker can employ the same technologies in his search for the right employer.

New advances in technology have given job hunters hundreds of new resources. Electronic resume and employment databases, job hunting software, and the Internet are just some of the innovations that have made it easier than ever before to write high-quality resumes, make industry contacts, and discover job openings.

The *Adams Internet Job Search Almanac, 6th Edition* is designed to prepare you to find a job in the information age. Within these pages, you will find hundreds of resources to help with every aspect of your job hunt, from preparing your resume and finding job openings to preparing for electronic job interviews. Regardless of your technological expertise, you will find an abundance of valuable information.

You can approach this book in two different ways. One option is to read it cover to cover so that you learn about the full spectrum of electronic job hunting possibilities. A second option is to use this book as a handy reference guide in order to find resources of particular interest, such as the Web address for a job hunting site that specializes in health care jobs.

The heart of this book is the description of hundreds of Web sites with current job listings you'll find in Chapters Three, Four, and Five. Here's a brief explanation of the information included for each site:

- **Number of job listings** is listed as a general approximation, as the number of job listings will continually fluctuate.
- **Types of jobs** indicates, in general terms, in which fields or job categories you are likely to find job listings.
- **Locations of jobs** tells you in which countries, states, or cities job listings can be found.
- **Frequency of updates** shows how often job listings are added to the database.
- **Search by** shows you how the database can be searched. Most sites allow you to search by keyword; some also allow searches by some combination of job category, job type, location, company, or keywords. *Job category* refers to a search by the sort of work the jobs require, such as administrative, technical, or media. *Job type* searches may allow you to look for internships, contract positions, full- or part-time jobs, co-ops, and telecommuting positions.
- **Resume database available** indicates that the site accepts resumes for posting.
- **Employer profiles available** means that the site lists information on specific employers.
- **Costs for job seekers** and **costs for employers** indicate applicable fees for using a service. Most job sites are free for job seekers, though many charge a fee to employers for posting open positions.

- **Other key features** tells you about career resources, besides job listings, that are available on the site.
- **Comments** is our impression of a site and its resources, and other relevant information.

Note: When we were unable to determine information within a reasonable degree of accuracy, the field was omitted from the profile.

Why Hunt for Jobs on the Internet?

Looking for a new job is rarely a pleasurable activity, but new advances in technology can help ease some of the stress normally associated with job hunting. With all the new resources available, relying only on the Sunday newspaper or old college friends to find job leads is no longer necessary. Internet job hunting opens a whole new avenue of contacts and opportunities—areas that were previously hidden or otherwise unavailable to the general public. The following are some additional reasons to add electronic resources to your job hunting arsenal:

- An understanding and knowledge of computers is the most sought after skill in new employees. Using electronic resources to find a job—even something as simple as e-mailing your resume to a company—is an easy way to demonstrate how computer savvy you are.
- Submitting your resume to an electronic resume database or posting your resume online will put your skills on display for the thousands of hiring managers and human resources professionals who regularly search these databases. This widespread exposure makes you a potential candidate for thousands of job openings that are *never* advertised.
- By using electronic business directories, either online or on CD-ROM, you can precisely identify those companies that hire employees in your field and with your background. These databases also contain enough company information to give you a good indication of whether a particular company is right for you.
- Not only are the Internet and commercial online services available to job hunters 24 hours a day, seven days a week, but their national and international scopes are ideal for job hunters considering relocating to another city, state, or country.

Electronic Job Hunting Resources

Job hunters with online access have a vast selection of resources from which to choose. There are hundreds of services available that can help you with all aspects of the job hunt, including networking, researching companies, posting resumes, and—most importantly—finding job listings.

In addition to the Internet, there are various electronic resources that can help speed up the job search process. Following are some more ideas to help you incorporate electronic technologies into your job search:

- **Write an electronic resume.** Having an electronic resume is virtually a necessity in today's job market. An electronic resume is simply a resume that is stripped of formatting, making it easy for a computer to read. Once you prepare an electronic resume, you can submit it to an electronic resume database, or simply mail it out to your target employers via e-mail.
- **Research employers through commercial business databases.** Developing a target list of potential employers and researching a company in-depth for a job interview have become much simpler, thanks to electronic business databases such as the JobBank List Service.
- **Use job hunting software.** Products such as *Adams Job Interview Almanac and CD-ROM* and *WinWay Resume* offer a variety of electronic job hunting assistance. With the help of these and other programs, you can easily create a professional-quality resume and organize your contacts. You can also prepare for a job interview, often with a video interview tutorial, complete with sample questions and answers.
- **Prepare for computer-assisted job interviews and assessment tests.** With many companies, your first interview may well be with a computer, not a person. As impersonal as they sound, computer-assisted job interviews seem to be the wave of the future, especially in companies that hire large volumes of entry-level employees. Similarly, computerized assessment tests examine your skills, personality, and integrity in order to determine how well you will fit with a particular job. Together, these two programs attempt to raise the quality of employees and lower turnover by ensuring that the employee fits the job.

Where to Begin

Now that you understand the benefits of an electronic job hunt, you will need some basic equipment; namely, a computer, a modem, and an Internet connection. If you're a student, you should be able to connect through your school's computer laboratory. Other places you can gain Internet access—if you don't already have a home connection—include local libraries and cyber cafes. If you have decided to purchase a computer and to connect from home, you'll be faced with several choices.

You have two basic choices of computers: a Macintosh or a PC-compatible machine. Macintoshes are much less common than PCs, and if you decide to buy one, you will have far fewer choices in terms of hardware, accessories, and software. A Macintosh with a System 8 or later operating system and a minimum of 32 MB of memory is a solid choice. For a PC, buy at least a Pentium processor. Also, you'll want a Windows 97 or more recent operating system, as well as at least 32 MB of memory. A CD-ROM drive comes standard on most new computers; you'll need one if you want to use any job hunting software.

As for modems, get the best and fastest modem that you can afford, which currently means at least a 56.6 Kbps modem. Anything slower, such as a 28.8 Kbps modem, could drive up your phone bills (if you're accessing through a long-distance number), and using graphically rich services will be painfully slow. With modems, quality matters as much, if not more, than speed. A high-quality modem has the ability to detect and correct errors in your phone line and connection.

Most new computers already come equipped with an internal modem, but if you have an older computer, you'll need to purchase one separately. You can choose from either an internal or external modem.

If you intend to be working online often, you may want to consider installing an extra telephone line to connect to your modem. You can use your regular phone line, but you may, depending on your modem software, need to turn off any special features, such as call waiting, before you go online.

Next, you must decide whether you want to use a direct Internet connection or a commercial online service. (Remember, commercial online services also provide full Internet access.) Many newcomers choose a commercial online service, mainly because of the wide range of services offered and their ease of use. Subscribing to a commercial online service can be as easy as installing the software. On average, expect to pay about $20 to $25 per month for unlimited usage with a commercial online service.

A direct Internet connection is generally the choice of experienced users who are more inclined to know the subtleties and nuances of the Internet. You can buy Internet starter kits at a computer store, or look in the phone book for "Internet Service Providers" for instructions on how to sign up. Generally, a direct Internet connection is less expensive than a commercial online service, costing anywhere from $10 to $20 per month for unlimited usage.

A Word of Caution

When people think of the many places where they can obtain free Internet access, work is often one place that comes to mind. Please note that searching for a job online while at work—even after hours—is completely unethical. Aside from being a risky undertaking, you are spending company time and money for personal advancement—an activity that is not looked upon favorably by any employer, present or future.

One Final Note

We recommend using the resources described in this book as a complement to your other job hunting methods. In other words, don't stop doing what has given you success in the past. Not everyone will want to, or should, use all the services mentioned. Instead, this book will help you determine which resources best meet your job hunting needs so that you can start down the road to career success!

CHAPTER ONE

THE INTERNET & GETTING ONLINE

Following the Soviet Union's launch of *Sputnik* in 1957, the Advanced Research Projects Agency (ARPA) was formed by the Department of Defense to examine the future use of computer technology in both military and scientific applications. ARPA immediately began lobbying for future computers to be designed with more interactivity. It was their view that computers would be most beneficial as communications devices, rather than as mathematical machines. In 1969, ARPANET, the Internet's predecessor, was developed. By the late 1980s, the government began encouraging commercial use of the Internet. Thus, what was once an exclusive playground for academics and high-level government workers has grown into an international network of millions of users, with thousands more signing on every day.

Online Strategies

Whether you choose a direct Internet connection or a commercial online service, take some time to become familiar with the service and the resources it offers. Check out some big career Web sites found in Chapter Three. Lurk in a few discussion groups to get a sense of what they are really about. In addition to familiarizing yourself with a service, this process will give you a good sense of how long it takes to find what you want online, so you'll be able to manage your time more efficiently.

If speed becomes an issue, try going online during off-peak hours, either in the early morning or late at night. Services experience less traffic at these times, so it can be much easier and faster to get through.

It's also a good idea to know what you want to accomplish before you go online. Have an agenda prepared, complete with keywords to search for and names and addresses of sites you want to visit. One of the most frustrating things about the Internet is how easy it is to get sidetracked; having a plan will help lessen the chance that you'll spend half your allotted time online in a discussion group chatting about the latest blockbuster.

A Variety of Methods Works Best

While enough cannot be said regarding the benefits of Internet job hunting, it's important to continue traditional job hunting methods, such as attending professional seminars, tapping into your network of contacts, and contacting employers directly. The rule of never relying on only one method to find a job still holds true.

At the same time, resources such as job hunting software and electronic business databases can actually help you with a traditional job search. For example, a resume-writing program can help you write a lively, professional-quality resume that is sure to get you noticed, and an employer database on CD-ROM can help you locate potential employers, who you can then contact through traditional methods.

Internet Service Providers

Typical ISPs offer customers modem dial-up access. The better ones also offer an array of technical support both on- and off-line. The type of Internet access an ISP offers ranges from basic analog modem access to DSL (digital subscriber line), and even wireless. The primary differences between these types of services are speed and cost.

Dial-up Services

Basic dial-up services connect customers through analog modems. This type of service is the slowest, but cheapest around. Generally, this access is fine for job-seeking purposes. Costs range from free to about $25/month. Free services, as you may have guessed, are often criticized for having low-quality access and poor technical support. In addition, free services often generate revenue by bombarding their members with ad banners. Some even track their users' Internet usage and sell the information to marketing companies. Still, if cost is an issue, employing the help of one of these services may be worth the aggravation. A directory of free ISPs can be found at **www.freedomlist.com.**

As for dial-up services that cost money, the range in price primarily reflects the amount of time users are allowed, the quality of service and technical support, and whether or not users are given space for a Web page. For $25 a month, it is possible to get unlimited access and about five megabytes of space for a Web site. *Boardwatch* magazine (located at **www.ispworld.com**) offers extensive news on the range of ISPs out there and maintains an online directory of Internet service providers on their Web site. The ISP directory also includes information on broadband access and Web hosting.

DSL

Digital subscriber lines offer Internet access up to fifty times faster than a standard modem. DSL, also known as ADSL, has many other advantages, including a dedicated line, meaning you are always connected when your computer is on. DSL signals can be sent without tying up any phone lines. Many DSL services also offer their members dial-up service for when they are on the road.

The biggest drawbacks of DSL accounts are cost and availability. DSL access for residential subscribers starts at about $50/month, and can be as much as $100/month depending on location and services desired. Most DSL providers will give out or loan out most of the necessary software and hardware for getting the service up and running; however, be cautious of hidden costs. The start-up software and equipment can run up to $500. The other drawback of DSL is its range. DSL works by sending a digital signal over existing phone lines, which weren't exactly designed for this purpose. As a result, the digital signal sent begins to break up almost immediately. Generally, two miles is the maximum distance a DSL modem can be from the central telephone office. Right now, DSL is available in most large cities and is constantly popping up in smaller cities and suburban areas. Check out **www.dsl.com** for extensive information on DSL technology and services.

Cable and Wireless Services

Cable modem access has been available to residential customers for a few years now, with mixed results. The biggest issue customers have is the "shared line" access they receive. This means that the more people using the service at the same time, the slower the connection will be.

On the plus side, cable access is usually a little cheaper than DSL; about $45 per month is not uncommon (most services offer special deals for customers subscribing to both cable television and the Internet). If you are interested in this type of service, your best bet would be to ask your current cable provider if they offer Internet access and if they have any special promotional offers.

Wireless Internet access seems to be the next big wave. Services range from a few Kbps (useful for little more than sending and checking e-mail) to speeds that can exceed DSL. Wireless access typically stems either from an existing wireless phone service plan or from a traditional ISP with special wireless capabilities. One issue to consider with wireless service is that users are often faced with pricey connection charges.

Commercial Online Services

The boundaries between commercial online services, ISPs, and other online businesses become hazier with each passing year. All major commercial online services not only offer extensive Internet access, but also market it as their primary service. Many "basic" Internet service providers now offer extensive tech support and online resources beyond providing simple bandwidth. The only sure thing is that the most popular and most successful online companies are the ones crossing boundaries and offering new and innovative services to their customer base.

Generally speaking, commercial online services provide Internet access, along with various membership services and resources not available to the general Internet community. These include financial and corporate information, technical support, online messaging systems and discussion groups, and various educational and entertainment venues. Memberships have generally been more expensive than the more basic Internet providers, but the gap is closing. Most commercial online services were developed in the 1980s, long before the Web was available; the services primarily targeted families and businesses. Even now, many families prefer the use of commercial online services, which offer filters to block young users from access to unsuitable material on the Web. Commercial online services also offer a more user-friendly platform, making it the ideal starting place for technical neophytes. It is not uncommon for people to start off with a popular commercial online service and after mastering the basics of use, move on to a standard ISP.

The Major Players

America Online
800-827-6364
www.aol.com

The largest commercial online service with more than 32 million members, America Online is well known for its wide range of home and leisure activities for the entire family. In addition to its own community, its company (AOL Time Warner) operates CompuServe, the Netscape Navigator and Communicator browsers, and AOL MovieFone, along with a multitude of other media ventures. Since the creation of the online Career Center in 1989, America Online has been the leader among commercial online services in terms of the resources it offers for job hunters. Prices range from about $5 to $25 a month.

AOL subscribers get e-mail accounts, free Web pages, and access to a variety of great chat sites and virtual shopping malls. Other membership perks include discounts on virtually every consumer item, wireless Internet, credit protection, and long-distance service. Remember to check out each service before signing on; many of them have fees in addition to membership requirements.

AOL's Job Hunting Resources:

AOL Careers and Work Channel
Keyword: Jobs

Legal Information Network
Keyword: LIN

The Teacher's Lounge
Keyword: Teacher's Lounge

The Writers Club
Keyword: Writers

CompuServe
800-848-8990
www.compuserve.com

CompuServe was purchased by what is now AOL Time Warner in 1998, yet it remains a separate and distinct service. Most of CompuServe's 2.8 million subscribers are businesses and professionals. CompuServe has by far the best collection of business resources available online, including dozens of business-related databases. While CompuServe does have services devoted to job listings, its strengths lie in its research capabilities and professional forums. CompuServe offers members complete Internet access, including a Web browser, so subscribers can access career-related newsgroups and Web sites. Over 700 special groups covering most industries allow members to gather and exchange information. CompuServe offers plans ranging from $9.95 a month for five hours of access to $24.95 a month for unlimited access.

CompuServe's Job Hunting Resources:

Broadcast Professionals Forum
Go: BPForum

Health Professionals Forum
Go: MedSIG

Career Management Forum
Go: Careers

Media Professionals Forum
Go: MediaPro

CompuServe Classifieds
Go: Classifieds

Military Forum
Go: Military

Computer Programmers
Go: Devappforum

Photo Professionals
Go: Photopro

Dun's Electronic Business
Directory
Go: Dunsebd

Writers Forum
Go: Writers

Education Forum
Go: Edforum

The Microsoft Network
800-373-3676 (800-FREE-MSN)
www.msn.com

Owned and operated by the Microsoft Corporation, The Microsoft Network was introduced in 1995. MSN's Career Center offers job seekers free information on important topics concerning the job hunt. Various articles and statistical information can also provide some helpful insight. Frequent MSN promotions allow for up to six months of free access. Memberships generally run just over $20 a month for unlimited dial-up usage and about $40 a month for unlimited broadband access. Microsoft's online services can be obtained free of charge just by visiting the Web site.

Prodigy
800-776-3449
www.prodigy.com

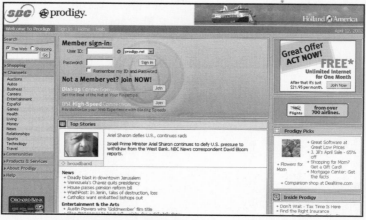

Founded in 1990 as a joint venture between Sears, Roebuck & Co. and IBM, Prodigy had been steadily declining throughout the late '90s. Since then, Prodigy has undergone a makeover and has grown to over 3.6 million members, making it one of the fastest growing of the major providers. Dial-up costs range from about $10 to $22 a month, with discounts for long-term commitments. DSL is available for about $50 per month.

Deciding on a Service

As the World Wide Web grows, commercial online services are becoming hard-pressed to offer unique services that cannot be found elsewhere on the Web. Online advertising has become a big business, allowing new Web sites to start up and offer an extensive array of services for free, profiting solely through advertising revenues. The greatest appeal of commercial online services is the online communities they offer. Networking forums, newsgroups, and chat rooms offered are available only to paying members, creating a more amicable environment. The best thing to do may be to go to the services, sign up for the free trials, and then decide which option suits your needs best.

CHAPTER TWO
THE ELECTRONIC RESUME

In an Internet-assisted job hunt, you will need more than just the traditional paper resume. As more and more companies are relying on applicant tracking systems to process and sort employment applications, and online databases to fill positions, creating a computer-friendly resume is of the utmost importance. Whether you're applying to a company that uses automated tracking systems, or paying to have your resume uploaded onto an electronic employment database, your resume must be in a format easy for a computer to recognize and interpret.

This chapter is an overview of alternative resume formats, focusing on scannable and Internet-friendly resumes, which allow job seekers to market their resume to thousands of employers with relatively little effort.

While electronic resumes are becoming more important in the job market, this does not mean that the traditional paper resume has become obsolete. Although many companies may advertise job openings on the Internet, some may request that resumes be mailed or faxed. As good a resource as the Internet can be in finding job listings, you will still come across job leads through other sources that may only provide you with a mailing address. Also, nothing spells competence more than a job seeker arriving at an interview completely prepared. Bringing along a neat copy of your resume to an interview is just one part of proper etiquette. Therefore, while you work to create a computer-friendly resume, you should continue to update your traditional one, because you never know when you'll need it.

Scannable Resumes

Traditional resumes target people, using action verbs and a clean, organized format. Scannable resumes target computers, using keywords (typically nouns) and very little formatting to grab the computer's attention. The goal of the scannable resume is to be so full of keywords and information that various searches will call you up as a possible match.

This is basically how it works: Your resume is fed into a scanner. Using optical character recognition (OCR) technology, the scanner "reads" your resume, recording important information like your name, address, and skills. This information is then filed into a database. When a position becomes available, the hiring manager is able to execute a search of the database by identifying certain keywords and receives a list of possible candidates.

One of the benefits of this technology is that since a computer is unbiased, each resume will be treated objectively. Also, because you're sending the resume for general employment, you can market your resume to potentially thousands of employers. Finally, you only need to send in your resume once, and it will continue to get exposure for months to come without additional effort on your part.

Disadvantages to this technology are that a computer will only look for resumes according to the criteria supplied by the recruiter. This tends to put recent college graduates or those switching careers at a disadvantage, since these job seekers are less likely to have as many keywords included in their resumes. Borderline candidates may be passed over by a computer search because they only have six out of ten desired keywords. These same candidates may have been brought in for interviews if a recruiter noticed some special accomplishment or trait that was never considered previously.

There is also the technology factor to consider. Even with new advances in computer scanner and optical character recognition software, there are still limitations. A small fold or a stain caused after you mailed your resume could eliminate important keywords or make your entire resume unreadable. Similarly, an unrecognized symbol or unfamiliar abbreviation could be read as nonsensical text. The best advice is to be as cautious as possible and, if costs are not a factor, consider resubmitting your resume after a month or so.

Formatting

The key to a scannable resume is to keep it simple. The same formatting that makes your resume look sharp to the human eye can make it impossible for a computer to understand. Following are some basic rules concerning how to format your scannable resume:

- **Length.** One page is still ideal. You can use a second page if necessary, but make sure your name appears at the top of each page. Always use a separate sheet for two-page resumes.
- **Paper and ink.** Use standard, 20-pound, 8½" x 11" paper. Because your resume needs to be as sharp and legible as possible, your best bet is to use black ink on white paper. When attaching your cover letter, use a paper clip—staples and folds can cause a resume to be misread.
- **Font and size.** Decorative fonts are difficult for a computer to read. Use a standard font such as Helvetica or Times. Keep the font size between 10 and 14 point (10 point for Times is too small).
- **Style.** Boldface is okay for section headers, but not for your name and address. Using all caps can also distinguish certain text, but do not let any characters touch each other. Do not use italics.
- **Graphics, lines, and shading.** Do not underline or use vertical lines. The computer will try to read marks on your resume as text. Anything that is not text can be hazardous to your resume's transfer.
- **White space.** Keep things spaced out. If characters or words run into each other, the information won't be readable.
- **Printing.** Ideally, you should print your resume at a copy shop or on a high-quality laser printer. Do not photocopy or fax your resume.

Content

The information you include in your scannable resume does not differ much from a traditional resume; it's simply the manner in which you present this information that changes. Traditional books on resume writing tell you to include lots of action verbs, such as "managed," "coordinate," or "developed." Keyword searches of scannable resumes tend to focus on nouns, such as a degree held or a software program you are familiar with. Personal traits are rarely used in keyword searches by employers. Following is a list of the basic information you should include in your resume:

- **Name.** Your name should appear at the top of your resume, with your address on the line immediately below.

- **Abbreviations.** Most resume scanning systems will recognize common abbreviations like BS, MBA, and state names. Widely used acronyms for industry terms, such as A/R and A/P on an accounting resume are also acceptable. It is good practice to try and include both forms so that none of your skills are over-looked (try using the abbreviation in the keyword summary, then spell it out in your experience).

- **Keywords.** The right keywords and key phrases are critical elements in your scannable resume. For example, let's say an employer searches an employment database for a sales rep with the following keyword criteria:

  - sales representative
  - BS
  - exceeded quota
  - cold calls
  - high energy
  - willing to travel

  Even if you have the right qualifications, without these key-words, the computer will pass you over. Furthermore, different employers search for different keywords. Figure out the buzz-words that are common to your industry or job that describe your education, skills, and experience. You should be careful to place the most important words first on the list, since the computer may be limited in the number of words it will read. One way to determine these keywords is to read help-wanted advertisements for job openings in your field; figure out the terms employers most commonly use and see which ones you can apply to your resume. Executive recruiters who specialize in your field are also a good source for this kind of information.

- **Keyword summary.** This is an inventory of your qualifica-tions, usually written in a series of succinct phrases that imme-diately follow your name and address.

- **Career objective.** As with traditional resumes, including a career objective is optional. If you choose to use an objective, try to keep it general so as not to limit your opportunities. Also, you should include possible keywords in the objective as well. The more keywords your resume can hit, the more likely it is that you will get a call.

- **Experience and achievements.** Your professional experience should immediately follow the keyword summary, beginning with your most recent position. If you are a recent college graduate, you should list education before experience. Be sure that your job title, employer, location, and dates of employment are all clearly displayed.
- **Education.** This section immediately follows the experience section (for recent graduates, it follows the keyword summary). List your degrees, licenses, permits, certifications, relevant course work, and academic awards or honors. Be sure to clearly display the names of the schools, locations, and years of graduation. You should also list any memberships in professional organizations and associations.
- **Interests.** Many people make the mistake of wasting space by listing their hobbies and interests. Since this information is irrelevant, it's completely unnecessary.
- **References.** Don't waste space with statements like "References available upon request," or by listing the names and contact information of your references. If and when an employer would like to contact your references, they'll ask.

The Cover Letter Question

While a cover letter will not help you in the initial selection process, it can help distinguish you from the competition in the final rounds of elimination. If you've taken the time to craft a letter that summarizes your strongest qualifications, you'll have an edge over other contenders who skip this important step.

Your cover letter should reflect your strongest qualifications. If you're responding to a classified ad, try to use many of the same keywords that the ad mentions. And if you're sending your resume to a new networking contact, be sure to mention who referred you.

One of the surest ways to eliminate yourself form a job opportunity is to send in a cover letter or resume with spelling or grammatical mistakes. Before sending out any piece of information, be sure you double and triple proof it. Get a friend to do the same.

Make sure your cover letter expresses an interest in the specific job and company, and that it clearly outlines your qualifications. Succinct and well written, a cover letter should never exceed one page in length.

ELECTRONIC COVER LETTER

69 Pageant Drive
Cambridge, MA 02138
(617) 555-5555

September 3, 2002

Ms. Natalie Goldword
Controller
Any Corporation
1140 Bones Street
Boston, MA 02215

Dear Ms. Goldword:

This letter is in response to your September 2 advertisement in the *Boston Globe* for the position of Assistant Controller. I am very interested in the position and believe I have the qualifications you are looking for. Please consider the following:

- Over twenty years' experience in Accounting and Systems Management, Budgeting, Forecasting, Cost Containment, Financial Reporting, and International Accounting.
- Implemented a "team-oriented" cross-training program within accounting group, resulting in timely month-end closings and increased productivity of key accounting staff.
- MBA in Management from Northeastern University.
- Results-oriented professional and proven team leader.

These are only a few of my credentials that may be of interest to you. I look forward to discussing them with you further in a personal interview. Thank you for your consideration.

Sincerely,

Michael Simpson

ELECTRONIC RESUME

MICHAEL SIMPSON
69 Pageant Drive
Cambridge, MA 02138
(617) 555-5555

KEYWORD SUMMARY

Senior financial manager with over twenty years' experience in Accounting and Systems Management, Budgeting, Forecasting, Cost Containment, Financial Reporting, and International Accounting. MBA in Management. Proficient in Lotus, Excel, Solomon, Real World, and Windows.

PROFESSIONAL EXPERIENCE

COLWELL CORPORATION, Wellesley, MA
$100 Million Division of Bancroft Corporation

Director of Accounting and Budgets, 2000–present
Direct staff of twenty in General Ledger, Accounts Payable, Accounts Receivable, and International Accounting. Facilitate month-end closing process with parent company and auditors.
- Implemented "team-oriented" cross-training program within accounting group, resulting in timely month-end closings and increased productivity of key accounting staff.
- Developed and implemented a strategy for Sales and Use Tax Compliance in all fifty states with 100 percent compliance for both parent company and subsidiaries.
- Prepare monthly financial statements and analyses for review by management executive board.

Accounting Manager, 1987–2000
Managed a staff of six in General Ledger and Accounts Payable. Responsible for the design and refinement of financial reporting package. Assisted in month-end closing.
- Established guidelines for month-end closing procedures, thereby speeding up closing by five business days.
- Promoted to Director of Accounting and Budgets.

MICHAEL SIMPSON
(page 2)

FRANKLIN AND DELANY COMPANY, Melrose, MA

Senior Accountant, 1982–1987
Managed A/P, G/L, transaction processing, and financial reporting. Supervised staff of two.
*   Developed Management Reporting package, including variance reports and cash flow reporting.

Staff Accountant, 1980–1982
Managed A/P, including vouchering, cash disbursements, and bank reconciliation. Wrote and issued policies. Maintained supporting schedules used during year-end audits. Trained new employees.

Junior Accountant, 1977–1980
Assisted in general ledger closing. Monitored cash collections and accounts receivable.

EDUCATION

MBA in Management, Northeastern University, Boston, MA, 1987
BS in Accounting, Boston College, Boston, MA, 1977

ASSOCIATIONS

National Association of Accountants

Applicant Tracking Systems

Applicant tracking systems, or in-house resume databases, are used by companies to keep track of the hordes of resumes they receive. Many companies, especially large corporations, receive hundreds of resumes each week. Where once these unsolicited resumes may have headed straight for a filing cabinet, or even the trash, electronic applicant tracking systems now allow employers to keep resumes in an active file, in some cases indefinitely.

In-house resume databases function much the same way as a commercial employment database. A company receives your resume, either unsolicited, through a career fair, or in response to an advertisement. Your resume is then scanned into a computer, dated, coded, and placed into the appropriate file. Whenever there's a job opening, hiring managers submit search requests to the database operator, who is usually someone in human resources or information systems. The database operator performs keyword searches in order to find resumes that match the criteria that the hiring manager has provided. The resumes of those candidates who meet the criteria are forwarded to the hiring manager, at which point the hiring process continues in the traditional manner.

As previously discussed, companies prefer this new technology because it is more efficient, in terms of both time and money. The automated system cuts down on paperwork and subsequently lowers administrative costs. Also, in major cities like New York and Los Angeles, classified advertising can cost thousands of dollars. With efficient applicant tracking systems, companies can just dip into their established pool of candidates.

There's also less chance that your resume will get lost on someone's desk or in a filing cabinet. When resumes are received, they immediately get scanned and put into a database file. Providing that your resume was scanned correctly, you won't have to worry about your resume getting misplaced.

One strong advantage is that, before this technology, you had little chance of landing a job with a company if you were passed over initially. Now, with an electronic applicant tracking system, your resume is kept in the database, where the use of keyword searches puts you in contention for every job opening.

Electronic Resume Databases

How would you feel if you were told you could contact hundreds, even thousands, of potential employers with a single copy of your resume? Well, with the help of an electronic employment database, that is exactly what you can do.

In many ways, an electronic resume database is similar to a traditional employment agency: You submit your resume to a service, and the service begins working to find a job for you. However, with an electronic employment "agency," you are considered for every job request that comes into a company, thanks to the use of keyword searches. While each resume database service is different, it generally works as follows:

- You submit your resume to an electronic employment database service. Some charge a fee, usually less than $50. Some services will also send you a "professional profile" sheet to fill out. Similar to an employment application, these forms ask you to indicate your work experiences, skills, and other information such as geographical preferences or willingness to relocate. This form is used either in addition to, or instead of, your resume.
- Client companies call the service with job openings, and they give the database service a list of keywords and desired qualifications. Some services allow employers online access to the database so clients can do the search themselves.
- The service provides the client with a list of possible candidates. Again, how the candidates are presented varies according to the service. Some services provide candidate summaries, others provide the actual resume, while still others also include the additional information that the candidate provided on his or her "professional profile."
- The client company sorts through the list of possible candidates and contacts desirable candidates directly. Some services will call you before forwarding your resume or any information to the client company.

Electronic employment databases offer tremendous advantages to both the job seeker and the recruiting company. A job seeker can easily be exposed to hundreds of companies with only one resume at little to no cost. In the past, it would take hours of research to come up with the company names, addresses, and contact names of potential employers nationwide.

For employers, resume database services can potentially save hours of work. Instead of putting a costly job advertisement in the newspaper or a trade publication, and looking through the hundreds of responses, companies can contact a resume database service and let the service do the work for them. In effect, these services prescreen candidates. While no company relies entirely on this method, many companies use it as first step in the search for qualified candidates, often because the database will give them a better idea of the available talent pool. For instance, if a database search turned up only a few qualified candidates, the recruiter may re-evaluate the minimum qualifications and skills set for a given position.

Many job seekers are wary of resume database services because of issues of confidentiality. What if you submit your resume to a database service, only to have it land on your boss's desk? Many services offer safeguards to ensure this doesn't happen. Some allow you to submit names of companies to block from seeing your resume. Others will contact you to get your permission before forwarding your resume or employment profile to a company. Some allow you to join the database anonymously—that is, your name, company names, education, and any other identifiable characteristics will not be shown to prospective employers. Check with different services to determine their particular policies, including whether the employer will see your actual resume or just a candidate profile.

The following is a listing of selected electronic employment databases.

Note: Be sure to check with each service before sending your resume or any registration fees. With today's rapidly changing technology, procedures and fees can change.

CIRS (Computerized Internet Resume Search)

www.resume--search.com *(with two dashes)*
P.O. Box 182, Eola, IL 60519
877-447-2477
Fax: 630-372-6292

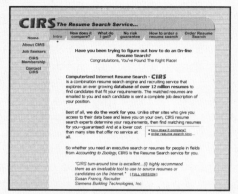

CIRS claims to have a database of over 12 million resumes, covering all services and locations. This service keeps resumes confidential until a match is made, and then informs the job seeker of the company's description and contact information. Job seekers are also allowed to submit a resume without a name (as long as other contact information is provided), to further enhance confidentiality. There is no cost to submit a resume to this service.

cors

www.cors.com
One Pierce Place, Suite 300 East, Itasca, IL 60143
800-323-1352
Fax: 630-250-7362

This service boasts of having almost 1.5 million resumes in their database. With more than 6,000 clients, the service matches about 200 jobs each month. The firm attracts clients in all fields, including computers, health care, finance, engineering, and communications. You can join this service for a one-time fee of $25. Once the service receives your resume, you will receive a confirmation letter in the mail that includes an identification number, which allows you to check on the status of your resume or make free updates.

Instamatch

www.instamatch.com
ProsperTech Group, Inc., 2900 W. Anderson Ln. #20–181, Austin, TX 78757
512-418-0303
E-mail: support@instamatch.com

Instamatch is a very basic resume-posting database service. It allows users to submit an ASCII text resume to their database through e-mail, which can then be viewed by employers that subscribe to their service. Using their InstaMail feature, employers can send a personalized message to any viable candidates via e-mail. At the time of this writing, there are over 6,000 resumes in the database, with an additional 200 to 400 added each week.

Your Resume Online

Over the past few years, the number of career Web sites offering resume databases has grown phenomenally. Many of the early sites that previously offered only listings of job openings now include resume databases as well. Several Web sites offer companies an annual membership, which includes unlimited access to resumes and job postings. The results heavily favor job seekers. Competition has prompted many of the sites to pay particular attention to the user-friendliness of their site. Most online services are free to the job seeker and many sites are scrambling to add new services and features to enhance both the job seeker's and the employer's experience.

Preparing a Resume for the Web

In addition to being read by scanners, resumes also need to be Internet friendly. In other words, your resume needs to be in a format that you can send to employers and online databases electronically, such as by posting it to a Web site or newsgroup, or through e-mail. Companies are increasingly requesting that resumes be submitted through e-mail, and many recruiters regularly check online resume databases for candidates to fill unadvertised job openings.

Online resume databases are very similar to electronic employment databases. Submitting your resume to an online resume database is an inexpensive method of exposing your resume to a large audience that includes thousands of human resources professionals and independent recruiters.

E-mailing your resume directly to potential employers is generally done in response to a help-wanted advertisement or simply as a method of direct contact. In fact, many companies now request that resumes be submitted through e-mail, rather than by U.S. mail or fax. Many job listings you find on the Internet, particularly for technical positions, include only an e-mail address for contact information. And with many companies, you can e-mail your resume directly into their in-house resume database. This eliminates the concern that your resume will be found unreadable by a scanner.

Preparing Your Resume as a Plain Text File

Whether you are e-mailing your resume or posting it online, it is important to make sure the resume will be readable. In general, copying and pasting your resume from any word processing program into the main body of an e-mail or on a Web site is acceptable. However, there are a few details to be aware of to make your resume as clear as possible.

- **Formatting.** Do not use words that are **boldface**, <u>underlined</u>, or in *italics*. Do not use any symbols or lines.
- **Alignment.** Make sure the entire resume is flush left.
- **Lines.** Keep your lines short. Many e-mail systems and databases will only allow 65 characters per line. Any lines that go over will either get cut off or jump down to the next line. Either way, it would make your resume look poor.

E-mailing Your Resume Directly to a Company

E-mail has several advantages over traditional postal mail. E-mailing your resume is quick, inexpensive, and efficient, for both you and your target company. Rather than spending time printing out a copy of your resume, addressing an envelope, and mailing it, you can simply send your resume with a few clicks of the mouse. This allows you to respond almost instantly to job listings online, as well as to ads you see in the newspaper. This means you can be among the first candidates a hiring manager evaluates. Many employers like e-mailed resumes because they cut down on paperwork and can lower administrative costs.

Unless a company specifies sending your resume as an attachment, the best way to go about e-mailing a resume is to paste it within the body of the e-mail message. If you are asked to attach the resume, you should attach it in a text format; for Windows 95/98/ME/XP, this would be in Notepad or WordPad.

Why Use an Online Database?

Why post your resume to an online database? In a word: exposure! Virtually all companies have an online presence, and the vast majority of today's professionals use the Internet in their daily routine. By posting your resume online, you are essentially marketing yourself to countless human resources professionals and hiring managers worldwide that are using the Internet. Online databases allow recruiters and hiring managers to search through large pools of candidates quickly and easily.

Another reason to use an online resume database is its reach. Online resources have stretched out their arms to the entire world. There are Web sites and newsgroups that target every market and job type. This allows job seekers who wish to find a job far from their current residence to take several of the first steps without ever making a phone call or leaving town.

After you e-mail your resume, wait a few days so you can be sure that someone has read it. Call or e-mail the company to confirm that your resume was received intact. As with a paper resume, an e-mailed resume may do little good unless you follow up to express your genuine interest in the company or the position. If you sent your resume to an individual, ask if he or she would like you to elaborate on any sections of your resume. Similarly, if you sent your resume to a general e-mail address, call the human resources department to check the status of your application. Assuming they have an in-house resume database and applicant tracking system, they should be able to tell you whether or not the e-mail was received.

Where to Post Your Resume Online

There are two Internet venues that work well for posting resumes: newsgroups and Web sites. Before you post anything online, remember to research the specific site or group to know exactly what you are getting into. Make sure you have the skills and experience that match the site's target job seeker. Pay particular attention to the location's privacy policy. Will your employer be able to access your information? Get a good idea of what sort of employers the site typically caters to. Do you really want your resume solicited to thousands of independent recruiters? This is a dream come true for some job seekers, a nuisance to others.

Usenet newsgroups are the most open forum on the Internet. Before posting your resume onto a newsgroup, spend some time reading through at least a few weeks worth of postings. Make sure the group accepts resumes! Make a note of the fact that Usenet is a completely open forum, where anyone has access to the information you post.

The World Wide Web offers a tremendous number of outlets for posting resumes. The following sites specialize in matching resumes with employers.

Note: Chapters Three, Four, and Five contain listings of hundreds of career Web sites; many of these sites include resume databases in addition to job listings:

CareerAvenue
www.careeravenue.com

Career Consulting Center
www.careercc.com

CareerEngine
www.careerengine.com

Hireweb
www.hireweb.com

HotResume.com
www.hotresume.com

InstaMatch
www.instamatch.com

JobDirect.com
www.jobdirect.com

ResumeBlaster
www.resumeblaster.com

Resume Broadcaster
www.resumebroadcaster.com

Resume Dart
www.resumedart.com

Resume Dispatcher
www.resumedispatcher.com

Resume-Net
www.resumenet.com

ResumeXPRESS!
www.resumexpress.com

Resume Zapper
www.resumezapper.com

Shawn's Internet Resume Center
www.inpursuit.com/sirc

US Resume
www.usresume.com

How to Post Your Resume Online

Most sites have their own specific instructions for entering a resume into their database. These instructions should tell you how long resumes remain in the database, how to update and remove your resume from the database, who has access to the database, and the fee (if any).

Some sites may require you to fill out personal information online, such as your name, e-mail address, and resume title, but most allow you to attach your own resume, or paste it in a specific area. Sites that offer personal profiles often have several fields for job seekers to fill in. In general, these fields can all be filled by cutting and pasting information from your resume.

If e-mailing your resume to a database, don't overlook one very important part of your e-mail: the subject line. The subject line sometimes ends up as your resume title; therefore, it's important that it gives an indication of your field and job title. Many people mistakenly type "resume" or even their name on the subject line. The subject line is typically the first information seen by employers scanning the database, and it is often the only information a recruiter will look at. It's important to be fairly specific on your subject line. Mention your profession, experience, and your location. For instance, "Financial Analyst – 3 Yrs. Exp. – CFA – Will Relocate."

Posting your resume on a newsgroup is similar to e-mailing it to a company. Like e-mail, a newsgroup has a subject line and a main message body. Newsgroups also offer the ability to include attachments and links. Newsgroups, however, are open for anyone to see. It is not advisable to post on a newsgroup that you are not familiar with. Many newsgroups shun the posting of resumes and will look down on the practice. Check out Chapter Seven on newsgroups for more information.

CHAPTER THREE

GENERAL JOB SITES
ON THE WEB

T he World Wide Web has become *the* place to look for jobs on the Internet, and with good reason. There are thousands of career resources on the Web devoted to job listings, with more springing up every day. While many contain general information regarding job hunting, a number of sites are more specialized, devoting themselves to one particular field, industry, or region.

Where to Find Job Listings on the Web

The popularity of the World Wide Web is due, in part, to its user-friendly interface. One of the best examples of this fact is to compare a Usenet newsgroup such as **us.jobs** with a Web site like Headhunter.net **(www.headhunter.net)**. A newsgroup shows only a very long list of job openings, and it is necessary to read each individual job title to get a feel for what the job is. But with Headhunter.net, a job hunter can simply enter in his or her desired job category and location, and the site's search engine will find jobs that match the criteria. Thus, a few clicks of the mouse produces a personalized list of jobs specific to the individual job hunter.

While interesting graphics might have been what first drew job hunters to the Web, its mountain of job-related information has kept them there. The Web has thousands of sites for job listings, and hundreds more for general job hunting resources, such as resume banks and employer databases.

The Web's job databases vary greatly in both the quality and quantity of job listings. We recommend starting with the all-purpose job hunting sites such as CareerWeb, Headhunter.net, Monster.com, and HotJobs. These are four of the largest and most popular job hunting sites on the Web, and they have thousands of listings for positions in all fields, in both the United States and abroad. Each also contains other helpful career resources, such as resume databases, employer profiles, and articles and tips to help you with your job hunt. Then try some of the other sites; you will probably find a favorite or two that contain the most job listings in your field.

One advantage of scanning the Web for employment opportunities is the quality of the job listings. Some job postings on the Web run as many as 500 words, a far cry from the minuscule want ad in your Sunday newspaper. These larger ads contain detailed information about the position, such as a lengthy job description, salary, and a specific list of required skills and experience.

In addition to the listings that follow, check out some job-related online meta-lists, which contain additional links to thousands of other online career resources. The Career Resource Center **(www.careers.org)** contains thousands of links to job resources on the Web. The links are broken down into categories, like financial services, or computers and engineering. NETability Inc.'s JobHunt **(www.job hunt.org)** and the Riley Guide **(www.rileyguide.com)** are two other superb sources of job-related resources on the Web.

Nationwide Sites (U.S.)

ABRACAT

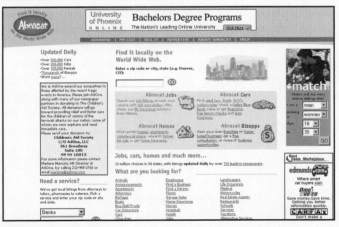

www.abracat.com
Number of job listings: Over 200,000

Types of jobs: All
Locations of jobs: United States
Frequency of updates: Daily
Search by: Experience; Job title; Keyword; Location; Skills
Resume database available: Yes
Costs for job seekers: Free
Other key features: "AdHound" e-mail notification service.
Comments: Ads are taken from newspapers around the country, so ad rates depend on which newspaper the employer initially places an ad in. A good site for finding local job listings, but make sure to check the date of the listing.

ADSEARCH

www.adsearch.com
Number of job listings: Over 4,000
Types of jobs: All
Locations of jobs: United States
Frequency of updates: Daily
Search by: Job category; Keyword
Resume database available: No
Employer profiles available: No
Costs for job seekers: None
Costs for employers: $25/ad running 60 days (up to 25 lines)
Comments: Adsearch is an online service provided by Miller Advertising Agency, a full-service firm specializing in print and online media advertising.

AMERICA'S JOB BANK

www.ajb.org
Number of job listings: More than one million
Types of jobs: All
Locations of jobs: United States
Frequency of updates: Daily
Search by: Job category; Keyword; Location: Military Occupational Code; Job number
Resume database available: Yes
Employer profiles available: Yes
Costs for job seekers: Free
Costs for employers: Free

Other key features: Links; cover letter services; a job search resource library.

Comments: This large database of jobs is culled from the combined job databases of 1,800 state employment offices. The listings contain detailed information including a job description and educational and work requirements. Many also contain the salary range.

AMERICAN JOBS

www.americanjobs.com

Types of jobs: All, with a focus on high tech

Locations of jobs: United States

Frequency of updates: Daily

Search by: Keyword; Location; Job category

Resume database available: Yes

Employer profiles available: Yes

Costs for job seekers: Free

Costs for employers: Different packages are available, and prices vary, depending on the degree of access sought.

Other key features: This site features a resource section with an extensive list of links, including toll-free airline numbers, relocation information, salary and resume tips, and recruiting news, just to name a few. American Jobs also offers a free e-mail newsletter.

Comments: American Jobs is one of the more popular job sites on the Internet, with an easy-to-read breakdown of search results.

BEST JOBS USA

www.bestjobsusa.com
Types of jobs: All
Locations of jobs: United States
Frequency of updates: Daily
Search by: Job category; Keyword; Location
Resume database available: Yes
Employer profiles available: Yes
Costs for job seekers: Free
Costs for employers: Contact site
Other key features: Newsgroup listings, articles from the monthly publication *Employment Review* online, and other career-related resources. The site's resume database offers a "resume masking" that prohibits employers from viewing your contact information without your consent.
Comments: An excellent site that provides a plethora of services and information. *Employment Review* offers a wealth of career advice to individuals and recruiting advice to employers. There is also information about Best Jobs Career Fairs, offered in more than 40 cities nationwide, as well as links to other employment-related sites. The site is maintained by Recourse Communications, Inc. (RCI).

BILINGUAL JOBS

www.bilingual-jobs.com
Types of jobs: All
Locations of jobs: United States and some international
Frequency of updates: Daily
Search by: Keyword; Language; Job category; Location
Resume database available: Yes
Employer profiles available: No
Costs for job seekers: Free
Costs for employers: $150 per 30-day posting, $600 for five 30-day postings, or $250 a month to search their resume database.
Other key features: Job search agent and a "jobs inbox" with listings that you have identified.
Comments: As the name indicates, this site primarily focuses on jobs that require a person to speak two or more languages. Free registration is required to post a resume or search jobs.

THE BLACK E.O.E. JOURNAL

www.blackeoejournal.com
Number of job listings: 250–1,000
Types of jobs: All
Locations of jobs: United States
Search by: Company; Job category; Keyword; Location
Resume database available: Yes
Employer profiles available: No
Costs for job seekers: Free
Costs for employers: Contact site
Other key features: Schedule of upcoming career fairs.
Comments: If you find a position that you are interested in, you must e-mail the journal with the job ID number. In addition, you must either mail or e-mail your resume to the journal so that it can be forwarded to the prospective employer.

BLACKVOICES.COM

www.blackvoices.com
Number of job listings: 250–1,000
Types of jobs: All
Locations of jobs: United States
Frequency of updates: Daily
Search by: Job category; Keyword; Location; Salary
Resume database available: Yes
Employer profiles available: Some
Costs for job seekers: Free
Costs for employers: Contact site

Other key features: Articles, columns, news, message boards, chat rooms, and other resources of particular interest to African-Americans.

Comments: BlackVoices is associated with the Careerbuilder Network.

BLACKWORLD

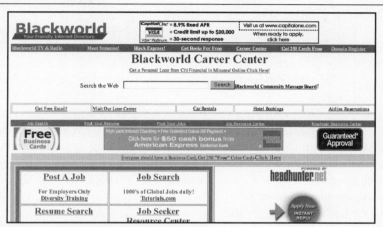

www.blackworld.com/careers.htm

Types of jobs: All

Locations of jobs: United States and some international

Frequency of updates: Daily

Search by: Keyword; Location; Job category; Salary; Employment type; Position type; Degree; Industry; Company

Resume database available: Yes

Employer profiles available: Yes

Costs for job seekers: Free

Costs for employers: Ranges from $200 for 30 days to $6,000 for a year for various services. See site for details.

Other key features: Business Resources sections that links you to areas such as "News," "Business Opportunities," and "Professionals"; the Global Media section furnishes a live audio feed from media outlets worldwide.

Comments: Powered by Headhunter.net.

BLUE RIDGE CAREERS ONLINE

www.blueridgecareers.com

Number of job listings: Over 10,000

Types of jobs: All

Locations of jobs: United States and Canada

Frequency of updates: Daily

Search by: Job category; Job type; Keyword; Location

Resume database available: Yes

Employer profiles available: Yes

Costs for job seekers: Free

Costs for employers: Start at $120/ad running 30 days. Additional services include "Post It Once," Web hosting, and an applicant tracking and job management program.

Other key features: "Notify Me!" e-mail notification service, and a confidentiality system that protects your contact information from employers.

Comments: It always feels like a hassle when sites *require* registration in order to use its best resources. However, by registering with Blue Ridge, job seekers are shown their account information including the number of jobs applied for on the site, a document manager to edit and upload applications and resumes, and the job seekers' resume status.

BOLDFACE JOBS

www.boldfacejobs.com

Number of job listings: Under 250

Types of jobs: All

Locations of jobs: United States and some international

Frequency of updates: Daily

Search by: Industry; Location

Resume database available: Yes

Employer profiles available: Yes
Costs for job seekers: Free
Costs for employers: $3/ad running for 30 days; resume searches are free.
Other key features: Links to other job, recruiter, and agency sites, as well as an Associations and Trade Organizations directory.
Comments: Although this is a small site offering far fewer listings than most job search sites, the Associations resource page can be very useful for job seekers interested in networking.

BRASSRING.COM

www.brassring.com
Number of job listings: Over 10,000
Types of jobs: All, with a focus on high-tech
Locations of jobs: United States and some international
Frequency of updates: Daily
Search by: Company name; Keyword; Location; Date posted
Resume database available: Yes
Employer profiles available: Yes
Costs for job seekers: Free
Costs for employers: Vary based on type of access and/or advertising.
Other key features: Schedule of job fairs; tons of career resources, including links to high-tech magazines.
Comments: While this is a good resource for the high-tech job market, the site's layout makes it somewhat difficult to navigate at times.

BUSINESSWEEK ONLINE CAREER CENTER

www.businessweek.com
Types of jobs: All
Locations of jobs: United States and some international
Frequency of updates: Daily
Search by: Company name
Resume database available: Yes
Employer profiles available: No
Costs for job seekers: Free, but requires registration.
Costs for employers: Vary depending on the company's size and needs.
Other key features: Personal Search Agent automatic e-mail service. As the online version of *BusinessWeek* magazine, this site offers extensive information on the economy and job market. Hundreds of past articles are archived through the "Selected Stories" link. Tools such as a cost of living calculator are also included.
Comments: Part of Leaders Online.

THE CAREERBUILDER NETWORK

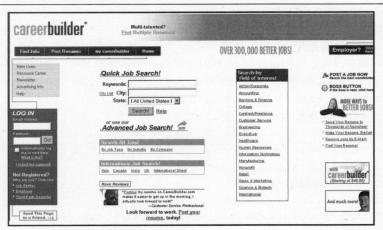

www.careerbuilder.com
Number of job listings: Over 300,000
Types of jobs: All
Locations of jobs: United States and some international
Frequency of updates: Daily
Search by: Job category; Job type; Keyword; Location; Salary
Resume database available: Yes

Employer profiles available: Yes
Costs for job seekers: Free
Costs for employers: Contact site
Other key features: Cover letter section, career planning information and advice, and links to each sponsoring company's Web site.
Comments: CareerBuilder is one of the most popular and expansive job search sites on the Internet.

CAREERCITY.COM, INC.

www.careercity.com
Number of job listings: Over four million
Types of jobs: All, with a focus on professional and high-tech jobs
Locations of jobs: United States and some international
Frequency of updates: Continuous
Search by: Keyword; Location; Job category; Other job search sites
Resume database available: Yes
Employer profiles available: Yes
Costs for job seekers: Free
Costs for employers: Contact site
Other key features: Offers a wealth of career information from best-selling job hunting and career books; free resume posting to a large, up-to-date resume database; and a search engine with links to tens of thousands of companies featuring job listings on their Web sites. This site's resources include a Salaries & Job Searching section with information on interviewing, resumes and cover letters, suggested reading, salary negotiation, and more. The Career Planning section covers topics such as career management

and self-assessment, and also features a "women's center," and the new start-a-business section. The site's innovative Diversity Job Center helps job seekers to successfully research companies with a proven commitment to diversity; the center also assists in helping companies to find qualified minority candidates for open positions. Also on this site are additional features such as an online career fair, showcasing selected companies, with direct links to all positions being advertised for each. Additionally, CareerCity.com contains detailed information on how to order career-related books and software, and a "Feature of the Day" column with career-related articles to help you with your job search.

Comments: CareerCity.com, Inc. provides a meta job search that allows candidates to search millions of jobs with one click of the mouse.

CAREER.COM

www.career.com
Types of jobs: All
Locations of jobs: United States and some international
Frequency of updates: Daily
Search by: Company; Job category; Keyword; Location
Resume database available: Yes
Employer profiles available: Yes
Costs for job seekers: Free
Costs for employers: Vary
Other key features: Links to company home pages; virtual job fair; and links to companies with entry-level positions listed.
Comments: Career.com is good for technical positions, and the number of positions in other areas continues to grow. All the job listings contain the dates they were posted, making it easy for job

hunters to gauge how long the listings have been floating around. The special area covering employment opportunities for new graduates is a great feature, as is the section featuring "Hot Jobs" of the week.

CAREER EXCHANGE

www.careerexchange.com
Types of jobs: All
Locations of jobs: United States
Frequency of updates: Daily
Search by: Job category; Keyword; Location
Resume database available: Yes
Employer profiles available: No
Costs for job seekers: Free
Costs for employers: Employers must contact Career Exchange for rates.
Other key features: People-Match e-mail service; the Conference Room offers a forum for career chat; and various career resources including relocation services and a salary calculator.
Comments: Jobs posted to this site are also listed on related newsgroups and sites.

CAREER EXPOSURE

www.careerexposure.com
Types of jobs: All
Locations of jobs: United States and some international

Frequency of updates: Daily
Search by: Industry; Keyword; Location; Job category
Resume database available: Yes
Employer profiles available: Yes
Costs for job seekers: Free
Costs for employers: $89 per ad
Other key features: CX Resources, including a list of business resource links for women.
Comments: A new feature, "Up Close & Virtual," is in the works at the time of this writing. It will feature in-depth interviews with industry experts from a variety of leading companies.

CAREERFILE

www.careerfile.com
Types of jobs: All
Locations of jobs: United States
Search by: Job category; Keyword; Location
Frequency of updates: As submitted
Resume database available: Yes
Employer profiles available: Yes
Costs for job seekers: Free
Costs for employers: $45 per month, $85 for three months, or $299 for a year.
Comments: Free registration required to search for jobs. This is a national network of locally owned career-related sites.

CAREERMAGAZINE

www.careermag.com
Types of jobs: All
Locations of jobs: United States and some international
Frequency of updates: Daily
Search by: Job category; Job title; Keyword; Location
Resume database available: Yes
Employer profiles available: Yes
Costs for job seekers: Free
Costs for employers: $100 per job per month; customized packages are also available.
Other key features: News and articles on issues relevant to job seekers; links to other employment-related sites.

Comments: CareerMagazine is part of the WorkLife Network.

CAREERMART

www.careermart.com
Number of job listings: Over 400
Types of jobs: All
Locations of jobs: United States and some international
Frequency of updates: Daily
Search by: Job category; Keyword; Location
Resume database available: Yes
Employer profiles available: Yes
Costs for job seekers: Free
Costs for employers: Starts at $225 for two weeks, with a variety of packages available.
Other key features: "My Career Mart," a resume-posting program that utilizes shopping cart technology to help pick out jobs a person is interested in.

CAREER NET

www.careernet.com
Types of jobs: All
Locations of jobs: United States and some international
Frequency of updates: Daily
Search by: Keyword; Location
Resume database available: Yes
Employer profiles available: No

Costs for job seekers: Free
Costs for employers: $35 per job posted
Other key features: "Featured companies" provides quick links to all of the positions being offered in those organizations. Other features include finding an apartment, salary and relocation tools, educational materials, personality assessments, and the "Career Coach" question and answer column.
Comments: Career NET is a strong resource for career information and job hunting tips, in addition to the job postings.

CAREER PARK

www.careerpark.com
Types of jobs: All
Locations of jobs: United States
Frequency of updates: As submitted
Search by: Job category; Company name
Resume database available: Yes
Employer profiles available: Yes
Costs for job seekers: Free
Costs for employers: Contact site
Other key features: Links to professional organizations, general career opportunities, diversity links, and a section focusing on students. This site also includes a link to a salary wizard, which will tell you how much you can expect to earn for a particular job in different locations.
Comments: Job listings do not indicate a post date, so you are unable to tell whether ads are brand-new or months old.

CAREER SHOP

www.careershop.com
Types of jobs: All
Locations of jobs: United States
Frequency of updates: Daily
Search by: Job category; Keyword; Location
Resume database available: Yes
Employer profiles available: No
Costs for job seekers: Free

Costs for employers: Costs range from $195 to $1,995 for various packages that include services such as job postings, resume searches, and applicant screening.

Other key features: Personal job shopper, an "Ask the Career Dr." column, and various other career resources, including links to relocation information, "resume blasting" services, resume tips, and a salary calculator. It also features "AutoHire RAS," a recruitment automation system that helps employers locate, track, and communicate with viable job candidates.

Comments: A good resource for job seekers and employers alike. This site is easy to navigate, and the e-mail service is beneficial to those who can't spend hours surfing the Web.

CAREERSITE

www.careersite.com
Types of jobs: All
Locations of jobs: United States
Frequency of updates: Daily
Search by: Job category; Location; Industry; Skills
Resume database available: Yes
Employer profiles available: Yes
Costs for job seekers: Free
Costs for employers: Free trial, then $25 per month, with discounts for ongoing commitments.

Other key features: Links to company profiles and job openings for specific companies. By filling out "MyProfile," you get free access to the job database, e-mail notification of job openings you'd be interested in, and you can post an "anonymous profile" that can be viewed only by potential employers you approve of through e-mail. Job seekers are also able to search jobs based on their personal profile, getting a list of openings ranked according to best match.

Comments: CareerSite has one of the best online resume/profile services for job seekers around. "MyProfile" is very user friendly and easy to access and edit. With one click, you can access a page to write in a cover letter to a specific ad and have your resume sent along in tow. You must register in order to use some services. The detailed job listings include information on job requirements and qualifications.

Career Women

www.careerwomen.com

Types of jobs: All

Locations of jobs: United States

Frequency of updates: Daily

Search by: Keyword; Location; Industry; Job category

Resume database available: Yes

Employer profiles available: Yes

Costs for job seekers: Free

Costs for employers: $89 per ad

Other key features: Links to news and resources for professional women.

Comments: Career Women is a part of the Career Exposure Network, which also includes Career Exposure, MBA Careers, and Diversity Search.

The Careers Organization

www.careers.org

Locations of jobs: United States and international

Resume database available: Links to sites that offer resume databases.

Employer profiles available: Links to sites that offer employer profiles

Costs for job seekers: Free

Costs for employers: Contact site for advertising information.

Other key features: Links to numerous popular job search sites; regional resources; links to books on Amazon.com; career media and newspaper listings; and links to major search engines, business news, employers, and career resources and research sites.

Comments: While this site does not contain job postings, it is a thorough directory covering many aspects of a job search. Whether you're looking for resume advice, an employment agency, a job in Saskatchewan, reading suggestions, or education resources, this site can lead you there.

CAREER JOURNAL FROM
THE WALL STREET JOURNAL

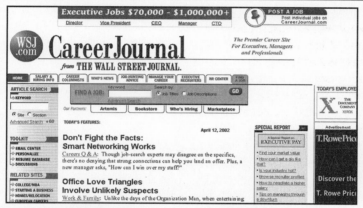

www.careerjournal.com
Types of jobs: All
Locations of jobs: United States
Frequency of updates: Semiweekly
Search by: Keyword; Job title; Job category
Resume database available: Yes
Employer profiles available: No
Costs for job seekers: Free
Costs for employers: $275 per ad per month, or $1,975 per month for unlimited access.
Other key features: Career resources including salary information, career columns, and links to executive recruiters; discussion groups; special reports; and an e-mail notification service.
Comments: An informative site backed by the reputation of the *Wall Street Journal*. The featured employers section is useful, but the multiple logos make it less appealing for users with slow Internet access.

CLASSIFIEDS2000

www.classifieds2000.com
Number of job listings: More than 200,000
Types of jobs: All
Locations of jobs: United States and International
Frequency of updates: Daily
Search by: Job category; Keyword; Location; Job type
Resume database available: Yes
Employer profiles available: Yes
Costs for job seekers: Free
Costs for employers: Contact site
Other key features: Includes Cool Notify e-mail notification service, career advice, research tools, and links to other job sites. Job seekers can search ads from employers, recruiters, or both. Includes contract positions.
Comments: A comprehensive "classifieds" site, offering all the services typically found in newspaper classifieds.

CONTRACTJOBHUNTER

www.cjhunter.com
Number of job listings: Over 2,000
Types of jobs: Contract technical, information technology, and engineering positions
Locations of jobs: United States
Frequency of updates: Hourly
Search by: Company name; Date posted; Keyword; Location

Resume database available: Yes

Employer profiles available: Contact information only

Costs for job seekers: Free to search jobs; other features, including resume services, require membership. Online membership is $20/year. A one-year subscription to *Contract Employment Weekly Magazine* is $50/year.

Costs for employers: $500/month (minimum three months) for unlimited ads. Various rate plans that include print ads are also available.

Comments: This site should be a definite for anyone looking for technical contract work, since it boasts that the advertised positions generally pay higher than other non-permanent work.

DIRECT INTERCITY DIRECTORIES

www.icdirect.com/joblink

Types of jobs: All

Locations of jobs: United States and international

Frequency of updates: As submitted

Search by: Job category; Location

Resume database available: No

Employer profiles available: No

Costs for job seekers: Free

Costs for employers: Free

Other key features: This site lists a number of international job opportunities, and includes an "Employment Wanted" category.

DIRECTJOBS.COM

www.directjobs.com
Number of job listings: Over 10,000
Types of jobs: All
Locations of jobs: United States and Canada
Frequency of updates: Daily
Search by: Date posted; Experience; Job category; Keyword; Location
Resume database available: Yes
Employer profiles available: Yes
Costs for job seekers: Free
Costs for employers: $150 per 30-day posting, $500 for unlimited 30-day postings, or $5,000 for unlimited job postings for a year. All packages include resume database access.
Other key features: Job search agent
Comments: You must post a resume in order to respond to job listings.

THE EMPLOYMENT GUIDE'S CAREERWEB

www.careerweb.com
Types of jobs: All
Locations of jobs: United States
Frequency of updates: Daily
Search by: Job category; Keyword; Location
Resume database available: Yes
Employer profiles available: No
Costs for job seekers: Free
Costs for employers: CareerWeb offers a variety of packages ranging from a single free 30-day posting to an annual membership package (contact site for details).
Other key features: Jobwire, a system that lets you interview online without a resume. This site also features career assessment tests; links to affiliates and other job sites; tips and advice on internships, resume writing, and the job hunt.
Comments: If you register your resume, you can respond to advertisements with the click of a button.

EMPLOYMENT 911

www.employment 911.com
Number of job listings: Over three million
Types of jobs: All

Locations of jobs: United States
Frequency of updates: Daily
Search by: Job category; Location; Keyword; Salary; Date posted
Resume database available: Yes
Employer profiles available: No
Costs for job seekers: Free
Costs for employers: $125–$174 per job
Other key features: Employment 911 searches over 350 other job sites to cull listings. The site's "Career Tools" section includes links to online education, relocation tools, and a career video featuring over ninety different careers. Relocation tools cover everything from a salary calculator to crime, insurance, and school information about communities across the country.
Comments: If you are a job seeker concerned with the sheer volume of job listings, this is the site for you. Since this site takes listings from other sites, however, search results may not be exactly what you were hoping for.

EMPLOYMENT WIZARD

www.employmentwizard.com
Number of job listings: Over 40,000
Types of jobs: All
Locations of jobs: United States
Frequency of updates: Daily
Search by: Job category; Keyword; Date posted; Location; Ad type
Resume database available: Yes
Employer profiles available: Yes
Costs for job seekers: Free
Costs for employers: Contact site
Other key features: Job search agent and a resources section containing information on finding a job, life in the workplace, and relocation.
Comments: Employment Wizard is a service that collects job listings from the classified sections of member newspapers. The network covers over 100 papers nationwide, and can be a helpful tool if you are looking for work in one of the cities or regions covered.

ExeCon

www.execonweb.com
Types of jobs: All
Locations of jobs: United States
Frequency of updates: As submitted
Search by: Industry; Location
Resume database available: No
Employer profiles available: No
Costs for job seekers: Free
Costs for employers: $250 for 90 days of unlimited job posting.
Other key features: E-mail service sends job seekers a list every ten to fifteen days of all new positions of selected industries added to the site.
Comments: This is a "no-frills" site that gets right down to business, quickly and effectively matching the job seeker with the job listings.

Exec U Net

www.execunet.com
Number of job listings: Claim 500–1,000 per week, and over 35,000 per year
Types of jobs: Executive-level positions
Locations of jobs: United States and some international
Frequency of updates: Daily
Search by: Industry
Resume database available: No
Employer profiles available: No

Costs for job seekers: Membership for job seekers is $135 for three months, $199 for six months, or $349 for a year.

Costs for employers: Free to post listings

Other key features: Newsletters, resume consultation services, and access to the site's salary database.

Comments: This niche site is by far the largest and best of its kind that we've come across.

FABULOUS CAREERS

www.fabulouscareers.com
Types of jobs: All
Locations of jobs: United States and some international
Frequency of updates: As submitted
Search by: Category
Resume database available: No
Employer profiles available: Yes
Costs for job seekers: Free
Costs for employers: Contact site
Other key features: Resume and cover letter advice, and a small directory of recruitment services.
Comments: This site takes an unusual approach (compared to the majority of job search sites) to finding a job in that it offers a directory of job categories, then employer summaries and links to the employment sections of their Web page. This is a good site for someone looking to work for a big company in a particular field.

FLIPDOG.COM

www.flipdog.com
Number of job listings: Over 500,000
Types of jobs: All
Locations of jobs: United States and international
Frequency of updates: Daily
Search by: Job category; Keyword; Location
Resume database available: Yes
Employer profiles available: Yes
Costs for job seekers: Free
Costs for employers: Contact site
Other key features: Like many other sites, FlipDog.com offers a 24/7 job hunter. It also contains a resource section featuring a monthly

"Best Places to Find a Job" report, links to events and seminars, advice and tips pages, a resource library, and resume writing and distribution information, as well as stress management tools and a training and tests section.

Comments: This is an excellent job search site, with not only a vast number of job listings, but also many useful tools and links to aid in your search for a new career.

4WORK

www.4work.com
Types of jobs: All
Locations of jobs: United States
Frequency of updates: Daily
Search by: Keyword; Location
Resume database available: No
Employer profiles available: No
Costs for job seekers: Free
Costs for employers: Job postings range from $25 to $75. Volunteer opportunities and internships are posted free of charge to employers.
Other key features: Includes job databases of regular full-time positions, volunteer positions, internships, and part-time positions, and an interactive agent that automatically matches job seekers with job listings. Also contains information on relocating, as well as links to numerous colleges and universities.
Comments: While it doesn't have the additional career resources (such as employer profiles and a resume database) offered by Monster.com, 4Work's jobs database is well worth the time of your search. Or better yet, if you register your personal profile— name, e-mail address, and skills—Job Alert! lets you know when an employer has posted an appropriate opportunity.

FORTUNE CAREER RESOURCE CENTER

www.fortune.com/careers
Number of job listings: Over 450,000
Types of jobs: All
Locations of jobs: United States and some international
Frequency of updates: Daily

Search by: Company name; Job category; Keyword; Location (All search categories operate via a keyword search for that particular field)

Resume database available: Yes

Employer profiles available: Yes

Costs for job seekers: Free

Costs for employers: Contact site

Other key features: Numerous articles and features, including the "Ask Annie" column and links to *Fortune* lists and services.

Comments: Formerly known simply as the Career Resource Center, this site is the result of a collaboration between *Fortune* magazine and FlipDog. While many of the site's options are restricted to *Fortune* subscribers, the jobs and resume databases, as well as the "View Employers" section, are open to the public.

FreeAgent.com

www.freeagent.com

Number of job listings: 5,001–20,000

Types of jobs: Freelance and contract, primarily high-tech positions

Locations of jobs: United States and some international

Frequency of updates: Daily

Search by: Keyword; Job category; Project type; Location

Resume database available: Yes

Employer profiles available: No

Costs for job seekers: Free

Costs for employers: Free to post projects

Other key features: "My e.portfolio" allows job seekers to create their own interactive resume/portfolio. The site also offers venues for networking and general business services information.

Comments: Interested candidates should register with the Web site in order to receive the many advantages that membership provides.

FreetimeJobs.com

www.freejob.com

Types of jobs: Freelance and contract jobs

Locations of jobs: United States and some international

Frequency of updates: Daily

Search by: Job category; Keyword

Resume database available: No

Employer profiles available: No

Costs for job seekers: Standard membership is free, and allows you to search for jobs. To bid on a job, though, you must be a premium member, which costs $10 per year.

Costs for employers: Free registration, and then $10 per posting per week.

Other key features: Registered users can receive free e-mail updates as new jobs become available.

Comments: Registration is required to use this service.

GeoWeb Interactive

www.ggrweb.com

Number of job listings: Over 10,000

Types of jobs: All, with a focus on geosciences, engineering, and computers

Locations of jobs: United States

Frequency of updates: Daily

Search by: Keyword; Location

Resume database available: Yes

Employer profiles available: Yes

Costs for job seekers: Free; for $59, job seekers can have their resume advertised on GeoWeb's Web site for three months and e-mailed to over 1,000 employers and recruiters (resumes can be posted to the Web site for free).

Costs for employers: $195 per ad, running 60 days. A quarterly membership rate is available for $1,490, and a yearly membership is offered for $4,500. Memberships include unlimited job postings and resume access.

Other key features: Links to hundreds of client company home pages; offers a variety of industry-specific newsletters that job seekers can subscribe to at no charge; an e-mail services that automatically notifies both job seekers and client companies of prospective matches.

Comments: Most of the site's in-depth services require a fee from either the job seeker or the employee. However, it does offer a good sampling of its services without charges.

GO JOBS

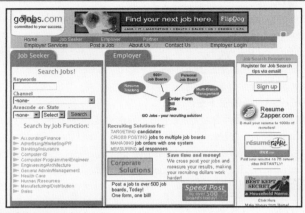

www.gojobs.com

Types of jobs: All

Locations of jobs: United States, with a large portion in California and Texas

Frequency of updates: Daily

Search by: Job category; Keyword; Location

Resume database available: No

Employer profiles available: No

Costs for job seekers: Free

Costs for employers: Contact site

Other key features: Also posts ads to classifieds pages and to partner sites.

HEADHUNTER.NET

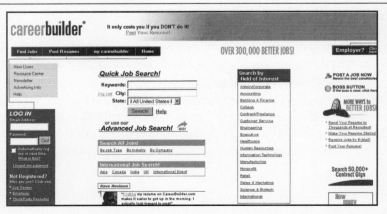

www.headhunter.net
Types of jobs: All
Locations of jobs: United States and some international
Search by: Education/Experience; Job category; Job type; Keyword; Location; Salary; Skills
Resume database available: Yes
Employer profiles available: Yes
Costs for job seekers: Free
Costs for employers: Standard job posting is $200
Other key features: The Resource Center offers interview assistance, financial advice, resume distribution, career assessment, training information, and related services.
Comments: Headhunter.net now charges employers for resume access. In the past, posting a resume on Headhunter.net was an invitation for intolerable spam, mainly from people who had no business using the site. With the new policy in effect, responses to your resume should be from reputable employers. Headhunter.net has also recently become part of the CareerBuilder network.

THE HELP-WANTED NETWORK

www.help-wanted.com
Number of job listings: Over 10,000
Types of jobs: All
Locations of jobs: United States and some international
Frequency of updates: Daily
Search by: Date posted; Keyword; Location; With or without abstracts
Resume database available: Yes
Employer profiles available: No
Costs for job seekers: Free
Costs for employers: At the time of our review, The Help-Wanted Network was running a "New Millennium" special, offering free job listings and resume searches for employers.
Other key features: "Other Resources" section links you to a limited number of career Web sites, company Web sites, and more.
Comments: In addition to direct job postings, this site uses a crawler to constantly search company Web sites for job openings.

HISPANIC ONLINE

www.hispaniconline.com/cc/

Types of jobs: All

Locations of jobs: United States and some international

Frequency of updates: Daily

Resume database available: No

Employer profiles available: No

Costs for job seekers: Free

Other key features: This site includes career-related articles from *Hispanic* magazine.

Comments: Hispanic Online is currently revamping their Career Center, in conjunction with Monster.com. This site promises to be a solid resource for Hispanic job seekers.

HOTJOBS.COM

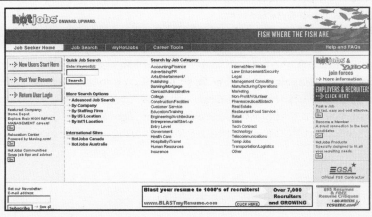

www.hotjobs.com
Types of jobs: All
Locations of jobs: United States
Frequency of updates: Daily
Search by: Keyword; Location; Job category; Experience level; Company
Resume database available: Yes
Employer profiles available: Yes
Costs for job seekers: Free
Costs for employers: $220 per ad for 30 days
Other key features: The career tools section contains a relocation center, information about how to assess the quality of your benefits and negotiate for a strong package, job tips, salary information including the latest news and a salary calculator, and an office humor page. HotJobs.com also provides links to companies' home pages.
Comments: A household name among career Web sites. HotJobs.com has done a good job keeping up with the industry standards and is a good starting point for any job seeker.

INTERNET CAREER CONNECTION

www.iccweb.com
Types of jobs: All
Locations of jobs: United States and some international
Frequency of updates: Daily
Search by: Keyword; Location
Resume database available: Yes
Employer profiles available: Yes
Costs for job seekers: Free
Costs for employers: Free
Other key features: Federal job information; links to other career Web sites.
Comments: While not the largest online job database, the Internet Career Connection claims to be the most experienced, and offers many articles related to career direction and job searching. This is a good site for individuals seeking career advice.

The Internet Job Locator

www.joblocator.com
Types of jobs: All
Locations of jobs: United States
Frequency of updates: Daily
Search by: Keyword; Location
Resume database available: Yes
Employer profiles available: No
Costs for job seekers: Free
Costs for employers: The cost for employers varies from free for basic access (sixth highest priority for job postings) to $10,000 per year for platinum access (highest job posting priority, resume searching, banner ads, and icon ads). See site for complete details.
Comments: This site is strictly devoted to job listings, and appears to no longer have links to other job hunting sites.

The Internet Job Source

www.statejobs.com
Types of jobs: All
Locations of jobs: United States
Search by: Date posted; Job category; Keyword; Location
Resume database available: Yes
Employer profiles available: Yes
Costs for job seekers: Free
Costs for employers: $50 per ad for 60 days. Resume access is available for $200 for six months.
Other key features: Over 30 state and area job source pages; *Fortune* 500 jobs; federal and state job listings; career-related news articles;

links to major search engines and local/regional/national online news publications; and a free weekly online newsletter.

Comments: This is a good site for people interested in positions being offered in a particular state.

JOB.COM

www.job.com
Number of job listings: Over 10,000
Types of jobs: All
Locations of jobs: United States
Frequency of updates: Daily
Search by: Job category; Keyword; Location; Job title; Salary
Resume database available: Yes
Employer profiles available: No
Costs for job seekers: Free
Costs for employers: Membership packages start at $99 per month.
Other key features: Resource section for job seekers, including links to resume writing and distribution services, other job boards, an online book store, self-employment information, and more. There is also a resource section for employers, which contains links to recruiting news, online job distribution, candidate assessment and screening services, applicant tracking programs, and more.
Comments: This appears to be a very popular site, with over 150,000 job searches and 30,000 resumes added to the system each month. This site recently merged with USJobBoard.com.

JOBBANK USA

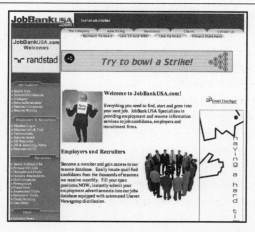

www.jobbankusa.com
Types of jobs: All
Locations of jobs: United States
Frequency of updates: Daily
Search by: Job type; Keyword; Location
Resume database available: Yes
Employer profiles available: Yes
Costs for job seekers: There is no charge to either view jobs or post a resume. This site also offers Resume Broadcaster, which, for a $79 fee, will send your resume to companies (more than 2,500 at the time of this writing) based on your preferences. Rush and re-send options are available for an additional fee.
Costs for employers: Contact site
Other key features: JobAgent e-mail notification service; career fair information; Usenet job-related newsgroups search; an online newspaper that features tips and job openings for international job hunters; and the Jobs Meta Search Page.
Comments: The real draw of this site is its Jobs Meta Search Page. Not only can you search the JobBank USA database, but you can also perform searches in the databases of several of the major World Wide Web job hunting sites, including Monster.com, CareerCity.com, and JobOptions all at the same time.

JOBDIRECT

www.jobdirect.com
Number of job listings: Over 500
Types of jobs: Entry-level for all industries
Locations of jobs: United States
Frequency of updates: Daily
Search by: Education level; Job type; Job category; Location; Work environment; U.S. work authorization status
Resume database available: Yes
Employer profiles available: Yes
Costs for job seekers: Free; however, registration is required
Costs for employers: $200–$375 for standard job postings. Quantity discounts are also available. Contact site for more information.
Other key features: Free resume database that notifies job seekers of opportunities that match their qualifications and criteria.
Comments: Focuses on recent and imminent college graduates, and matches resumes with entry-level job openings.

JOBFIND.COM

www.jobfind.com

Types of jobs: All

Locations of jobs: United States and some international

Frequency of updates: Daily

Search by: Company name; Job category; Job title; Keyword; Location; Salary

Resume database available: Yes

Employer profiles available: Yes

Costs for job seekers: Free

Costs for employers: Rates range from $100 per ad running one month to the Elite Charter Package, which, for $15,000 a year, includes unlimited job postings, resume access, a corporate profile with a link to the company's Web site, and three job banner ads.

Other key features: Listing of job fairs; an event calendar; current, related news articles; and MyJobFind, an e-mail notification service.

JOBHUNT.COM

www.jobhunt.com

Types of jobs: All

Frequency of updates: More than once per week

Employer profiles available: Yes

Other key features: Search online resume banks, newsgroups, company profiles, and jobs specifically in academics, medicine, science, and engineering; searchable database of recruiters; links to

University career centers, online reference material, and informative career resources.

Comments: We found this to be one of the most thorough and complete career sites on the Web. This site doesn't actually have a job or resume database, but the number of links to Web sites with those resources is amazing.

JOBOPTIONS

www.joboptions.com

Types of jobs: All, primarily managerial, technical, and professional positions

Locations of jobs: United States and some international

Frequency of updates: Daily

Search by: Job category; Location; Keyword; Company

Resume database available: Yes

Employer profiles available: Yes

Costs for job seekers: Free

Costs for employers: Rates start at $60 per ad running 30 days, to $7,900 for an annual unlimited plan.

Other key features: More than enough employer profiles to keep you busy for awhile; HR Tools covers a variety of human resource topics; e-mail services for both the job seeker *and* the employer— Job Alert notifies job seekers of new positions matching their criteria, while Resume Alert e-mail a list of possible candidates matching an employer's openings; and the CareerZone section offers tips on creating a resume, salary and relocation information, career news, and more.

Comments: Another very useful site, which is easy to navigate and offers more than simple jobs and resume databases. Especially true for this site is its emphasis on serving both the job seeker and the employer, making this a must-see site for people on both sides of the job search.

JOBS.COM

www.jobs.com
Number of job listings: Over 500
Types of jobs: All
Locations of jobs: United States
Frequency of updates: Daily
Search by: Keyword; Exclude keyword; Job category; Job type; Location; Salary; Company name
Resume database available: Yes
Employer profiles available: Yes
Costs for job seekers: Free
Costs for employers: $25 for part-time job post, and $129 for a full-time job post. Quantity discounts are also available.
Other key features: A "Communities" section with categories such as *military*, *healthcare*, *college*, and *diversity*; and "Tools and Resources," featuring a job search agent, salary comparison tools, education links, and a resource center.
Comments: This site features Online Resume (formerly Resumail), which helps users to create an online resume by allowing them to key in their information (experience, education, etc.), which the software automatically plugs into electronic format, ensuring a readable electronic resume.

THE JOB-SEARCH-ENGINE

www.jobsearchengine.com
Number of job listings: Over three million in the United States
Types of jobs: All
Locations of jobs: United States, Canada, and the United Kingdom
Search by: Keyword; Location; Job category; Salary; Date posted
Resume database available: No
Employer profiles available: No
Costs for job seekers: Free

Other key features: Resource Center lists and links to jobs sites, career services sites, and several specialized job sites.

Comments: This site searches over 120 other job sites to find potential matches. Sample searches for "engineering" and "computer programmer" pulled up 500 jobs (which appears to be the maximum number of returns that the site allows). **Note:** Some job listings may be duplicates.

JOBSITE.COM

www.jobsite.com
Number of job listings: Under 250
Types of jobs: Real Estate; Real Estate Finance; Construction; Architecture; Engineering
Locations of jobs: United States
Frequency of updates: Daily
Search by: Company name; Experience; Keyword; Location
Resume database available: Yes
Employer profiles available: Yes
Costs for job seekers: Free
Costs for employers: Contact site
Other key features: Real estate news; bookstore with links to Amazon.com.
Comments: Site requires registration for use.

JOBSJOBSJOBS

www.jobsjobsjobs.com
Types of jobs: All
Locations of jobs: United States
Frequency of updates: Daily
Search by: Job category; Keyword
Resume database available: Yes
Employer profiles available: No
Costs for job seekers: Free
Costs for employers: Vary, depending on the size of your company and how long the ad will run.
Other key features: Free e-mail; links to Web-based training classes; and an e-mail newsletter.

JOB SLEUTH

www.jobsleuth.com
Number of job listings: Over 4,500,000
Types of jobs: All
Locations of jobs: United States and Canada
Frequency of updates: Daily
Search by: Location; Job category; Job type; Keyword
Resume database available: Yes
Employer profiles available: No
Costs for job seekers: Free
Costs for employers: Contact site
Other key features: A nice career tools section containing resume, salary, and relocation tools; a reference checker; a career analysis program; and a free audio program featuring ways to get the job you really want. There is also a handy employer tools section, with links to a free resume bank, IT help, and a job posting site that sends available positions to over 1,000 Web sites.
Comments: Job Sleuth is a product of Infonautics, Inc., and is a member of their Sleuth series of sites.

JOB SNIPER

www.jobsniper.com
Number of job listings: Potentially over 1,000,000
Types of jobs: All
Locations of jobs: United States; Canada; United Kingdom
Search by: Keyword; Location; Web site
Resume database available: No
Employer profiles available: No
Costs for job seekers: Free
Other key features: Job search agent; and links to other career sites.
Comments: Job Sniper searches up to about two dozen other job search sites, resulting in a higher number of job postings per search, but will not necessarily result in unique returns.

JOBVERTISE

www.jobvertise.com
Number of job listings: Over 50,000
Types of jobs: All
Locations of jobs: United States and some international

Frequency of updates: Daily
Search by: Keyword; Location
Resume database available: Yes
Employer profiles available: No
Costs for job seekers: Free
Costs for employers: Free; advertising is also available. See site for rate card information.
Comments: Companies can use Jobvertise to set up jobs pages on their own sites.

JOB WAREHOUSE

www.jobwarehouse.com
Number of job listings: Over 5,000
Types of jobs: High tech
Locations of jobs: United States
Frequency of updates: Daily
Search by: Keyword; Location; Job type
Resume database available: Yes
Employer profiles available: Yes
Costs for job seekers: Free
Costs for employers: Contact site
Other key features: Job search workshop; and a job search agent.
Comments: Formerly known as PASSPORTAccess, this site focuses on technical candidates and recruiters. Job Warehouse allows you to view the entire list of jobs available at a particular company, visit the company's Web site, or see what the position's requirements are before viewing the listing.

LATPRO

www.latpro.com
Types of jobs: All
Locations of jobs: United States and international
Frequency of updates: Daily
Search by: Job category; Keyword; Language; Location
Resume database available: Yes
Employer profiles available: No
Costs for job seekers: Free
Costs for employers: Free

Other key features: Job search agent; salary and relocation information; a newsletter; a resume center; a "learn English" online course; recruiter tools; and more.

Comments: All jobs offered on this site require fluency in Spanish and/or Portuguese, in addition to English. The site is also offered in Spanish and Portuguese.

LYCOS CAREERS

http://careers.lycos.com
Number of job listings: Over 5,000
Types of jobs: All
Locations of jobs: United States
Frequency of updates: Daily
Search by: Keyword; Location; Job category; Full-time or Contract
Resume database available: Yes
Employer profiles available: Yes
Costs for job seekers: Free
Costs for employers: Contact site
Other key features: Links to online career fairs; a resume review service; "Career Coach"; advice from career experts; a job search FAQ; career clubs; relocation information; and links to the other areas and search tools from Lycos.com.

Comments: This is the career section of the Lycos search engine, giving job seekers the opportunity to access almost any type of information needed with just a few clicks of the mouse.

MBA CAREERS
www.mbacareers.com
Types of jobs: MBA positions

Locations of jobs: United States and some international
Frequency of updates: As submitted.
Search by: Industry; Job category; Keyword; Location
Resume database available: Yes
Employer profiles available: Yes
Costs for job seekers: Free
Costs for employers: $89 per listing
Other key features: Links to business resource sites.

MBA FREEAGENTS.COM

www.mbafreeagents.com
Types of jobs: Interim; high tech; and other business-related jobs for MBAs
Locations of jobs: United States and some international
Frequency of updates: Daily
Resume database available: Yes
Costs for job seekers: Basic membership is free; Network membership is $60.
Costs for employers: Prices start at $250 for a single full-time job posting for 30 days. Longer contracts with more options are also available.
Other key features: E-mail interaction between job seekers and employers/hiring managers; and a database of alumni members.
Comments: Membership is required for this job matching service for MBAs from top business schools. The 39 schools are members of the International MBA placement group. Applicants must meet one of the following: one to 15 years out of business school, 30 years of experience, or be an independent consultant. Job seekers who qualify should register in the members database, which is searched by employers.

MONSTER.COM

www.monster.com
Number of job listings: Over one million
Types of jobs: All
Locations of jobs: United States and international
Frequency of updates: Daily
Search by: Company; Job category; Keyword; Location
Resume database available: Yes
Employer profiles available: Yes
Costs for job seekers: Free
Costs for employers: $305 per ad running 60 days. Resume search costs vary.
Other key features: Career resource center featuring 3,000 pages of resume help, salary data, and industry information; free newsletter; "zones" for different experience levels and specific fields (such as Health Care, Technology, and dot.coms); expert job hunting and career advice; and a job search agent. There are also links to affiliated international sites like Monster Board UK.
Comments: Monster.com (formerly The Monster Board) is one of the best (and best known), most comprehensive job hunting resources on the Web. It is an easy-to-use, graphically entertaining site that provides job hunters with tons of valuable information. The job listings themselves are thorough, and if you have previously submitted your resume to the resume database, you can apply for positions with impressive ease. It's a true monster, too, growing all the time through partnerships with other job hunting sites.

NATIONAL AD SEARCH

www.nationaladsearch.com
Number of job listings: Over 10,000
Types of jobs: All, primarily managerial and technical positions
Locations of jobs: United States
Frequency of updates: Weekly
Search by: Location; Job category; Date
Resume database available: Yes
Employer profiles available: No
Costs for job seekers: $10 per block of 100 ads
Other key features: Resume exchange allows job seekers to create a resume with its own URL, giving job seekers a hyperlink to their

resume when e-mailing potential employers. The job listings are compiled from 60 newspapers from major U.S. metropolitan areas.

Comments: Job seekers can sign up for a free trial subscription.

NATIONJOB NETWORK

www.nationjob.com
Types of jobs: All
Locations of jobs: United States and some international
Frequency of updates: Daily
Search by: Education; Job category; Job type; Location; Salary; Duration; Company
Resume database available: Yes
Employer profiles available: Yes
Costs for job seekers: Free
Costs for employers: Starts at $150 for a two-page description for 30 days.
Other key features: A job search agent called P.J. Scout; a variety of specialty Web pages; and links to Web sites of many sponsoring companies (all of whom have current job openings posted).
Comments: Specialty pages enable job seekers to research companies in a particular employment category or geographical area. The "Community Pages" section offers current, local job information for much of the country.

NET-TEMPS

www.net-temps.com
Number of job listings: Over 50,000
Types of jobs: Primarily contract and temporary jobs
Locations of jobs: United States and Canada
Frequency of updates: Daily
Search by: Job category; Job type; Keyword; Location
Resume database available: Yes
Employer profiles available: Yes
Costs for job seekers: Free
Costs for employers: A single job posting is $95; membership packages with more options are available. Contact site for full details.

Other key features: Free job seeker desktop; career channels; articles; ask the expert; and various recruiter and employer links and services.

Comments: A good site with comprehensive job listings for those seeking exposure to recruiters' openings in a variety of fields. This site lists thousands of job listings from as many as 7,500 employment agencies.

RECRUITERS ONLINE NETWORK

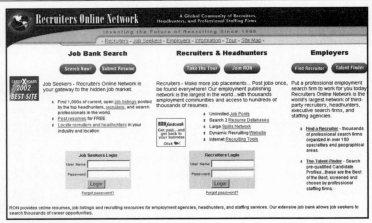

www.recruitersonline.com
Number of job listings: Claims to offer thousands of job listings
Types of jobs: All
Locations of jobs: United States and some international
Frequency of updates: Daily
Search by: Industry; Job category; Keyword; Location
Resume database available: Yes
Employer profiles available: Yes
Costs for job seekers: Free
Costs for employers: Contact site
Comments: This site is an association of recruiters. Recommended for job seekers willing to work with recruiters; this site is a strong option with potentially thousands of recruiters working on your job hunt.

SALUDOS HISPANOS

www.saludos.com
Number of job listings: Over 250

Types of jobs: All
Locations of jobs: United States
Frequency of updates: As submitted.
Search by: Job category; Company; Location
Resume database available: Yes
Employer profiles available: Yes
Costs for job seekers: Free
Costs for employers: $99 per ad running one month, or $129 for two
   months. Advertising opportunities are also available.
Other key features: Links concerning Hispanics; online job fairs; and
   a free newsletter.
Comments: Good site for Hispanic job seekers and recruiters or
   companies interested in diversity.

TELECOMMUTING JOBS

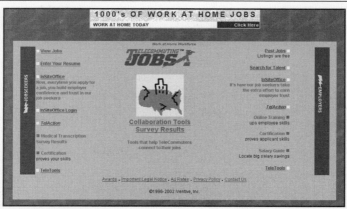

www.tjobs.com
Number of job listings: Under 1,000
Types of jobs: Telecommuting
Frequency of updates: As submitted
Search by: Job category
Resume database available: Yes
Employer profiles available: No
Costs for job seekers: Free
Costs for employers: Free; advertising packages are also available.
Other key features: "TelAction" news featuring issues relevant to
   telecommuters; "TeleTools" links to sites of interest to
   telecommuters.

Comments: This site features jobs targeting the "from home" worker, as well as some freelance job listings.

VALUEJOBS.COM

www.valuejobs.com
Number of job listings: Over 1,000
Types of jobs: All
Locations of jobs: United States and international
Frequency of updates: Daily
Search by: Job category; Location; Keyword; Salary
Resume database available: Yes
Employer profiles available: Yes
Costs for job seekers: Free
Costs for employers: It is free to post up to ten jobs for 60 days. If posting more than ten jobs, the cost is $5 per listing for 60 days.
Other key features: Links to career and resume services
Comments: Considering this site's ease of use and extremely low cost for employers, expect this site to grow in the coming months.

VAULT.COM

www.vault.com
Number of job listings: Over 10,000
Types of jobs: All
Locations of jobs: United States
Frequency of updates: Daily
Search by: Job category; Job type; Location; Keyword; Experience level
Resume database available: Yes
Employer profiles available: Yes
Costs for job seekers: Free
Costs for employers: $49 per job posting
Other key features: Research section featuring Vault reports and career guides; news; featured jobs; message boards; and a "why work for us" section written by employers.
Comments: Vault.com has increased its services since the last update, providing more options and tools both for job seekers and employers.

VETJOBS.COM

www.vetjobs.com

Number of job listings: Over 300

Types of jobs: All, with many middle management and teaching positions

Locations of jobs: United States and some international

Frequency of updates: Daily

Search by: Date posted; Job category; Keyword; Location

Resume database available: Yes

Employer profiles available: No

Costs for job seekers: Free

Costs for employers: Ranges from $120 for a single job posting to $6,000 for full membership for a year.

Other key features: Information and links concerning transition assistance, veteran resources, and veteran services.

Comments: Sponsored by the Veterans of Foreign Wars of the United States, this site is open to persons who have served in the U.S. armed forces, active duty, or the reserves.

YAHOO! CAREERS

http://careers.yahoo.com

Number of job listings: Over 100,000

Types of jobs: All

Locations of jobs: United States and some international

Frequency of updates: Daily

Search by: Company name; Job category; Job title; Keyword; Location; Salary; Employment type

Resume database available: Yes

Employer profiles available: Yes

Costs for job seekers: Free

Costs for employers: Starts at $200 for a single job post. Packages including multiple job postings and access to the resume bank are also available. Contact site for details.

Other key features: Resume tools; Job alert; Salary wizard; Executive center; and Career Communities.

Comments: Yahoo! is one of the most popular sites on the Internet, and in the same vein, this is a very popular job search site. It offers ease of use and the strong reputation of the Yahoo! name.

Sites for Students and Recent Grads

The following sites are aimed at those with little experience in the job market. Along with job listings, a number of these sites provide career and job search advice. Many of the jobs available here will be for entry-level or lower level positions.

ADGUIDE'S COLLEGE RECRUITER EMPLOYMENT SITE

www.adguide.com

Number of job listings: 500,000

Types of jobs: All

Locations of jobs: United States and some international

Frequency of updates: Daily

Search by: Job category; Keyword; Location; Date posted

Resume database available: Yes

Employer profiles available: Yes

Costs for job seekers: Free

Costs for employers: Job postings and resume access start at $125 each.

Other key features: Links to related sites; e-mail notification service; links to company e-mail addresses; financial aid information; and news and relevant articles.

Comments: This site focuses on students heading into graduation, or those who have recently graduated. Recruiters post jobs to this site for entry-level through experienced positions, as well as for part-time jobs and internships. Company information is provided through a partnership with WetFeet.com.

AFTERCOLLEGE.COM

www.thejobresource.com
Number of job listings: Over 900
Types of jobs: All
Locations of jobs: United States
Frequency of updates: **Daily**
Search by: Job type; Industry; Location; Keyword
Resume database available: Yes
Employer profiles available: Lists of companies (by category), with links to both their Web sites and available jobs.
Costs for job seekers: Free for basic use; $14.95 for the career assessment program.
Costs for employers: Contact site
Other key features: Career advice; the daily tip; the "Aftercollege Agent" which allows users to send the resume posted on this site to any e-mail address; a career assessment service; and an Alumni network that can put you in touch with other people who attended the same college that you did.
Comments: Aftercollege.com offers some unique services that should make it attractive to job seekers just out of college. As you might expect, the majority of the jobs are entry- and low-level.

THE BLACK COLLEGIAN ONLINE

www.blackcollegian.com
Number of job listings: Over 5,000
Types of jobs: All
Locations of jobs: United States
Frequency of updates: Daily
Search by: Company name; Keyword; Location; Job category
Resume database available: Yes
Employer profiles available: Yes
Costs for job seekers: Free
Costs for employers: $175 per ad for nonmembers. Membership plans that include unlimited job posting and resume searches are available. Contact site for details.

Other key features: Each job description has an option to e-mail a response to the ad, as well as a link to the employer's profile. This site also boasts a selection of channels covering career, education, and African-American issues of interest.

Comments: The online version of *The Black Collegian*, a magazine distributed to college career centers twice a year (the online version is updated regularly). Many of the jobs listed are from major corporations.

CAREERBUZZ.COM

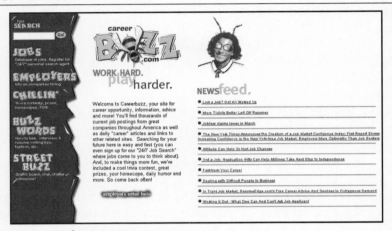

www.careerbuzz.com

Number of job listings: Over 2,500

Types of jobs: All

Locations of jobs: United States

Frequency of updates: Daily

Search by: Job category; Keyword; Location

Resume database available: No

Employer profiles available: Yes

Costs for job seekers: Free

Costs for employers: $25 per ad running 30 days. Bulk posting and customized packages are also available.

Other key features: Heavy focus on entertaining users with chat rooms, message boards, games, extreme-sports style design, and hints geared toward younger job seekers.

Comments: Most of the jobs are nonprofessional positions. However, this site gets high marks for catering to the entry-level/student audience.

COLLEGECENTRAL.COM

www.collegecentral.com
Number of job listings: Over 3,000,000
Types of jobs: All
Locations of jobs: United States
Frequency of updates: Daily
Search by: Location; Job category; Keyword; Salary
Resume database available: Yes
Employer profiles available: Yes
Costs for job seekers: Free
Costs for employers: Post jobs to up to 25 schools for $50 per month
Other key features: Campus news; issues; weather; article archives; and virtual career fair information.
Comments: You must submit a resume in order to use certain services. This site is powered by Careerbuilder.com.

COLLEGE GRAD JOB HUNTER

www.collegegrad.com
Types of jobs: Entry-level; Internships; Professional
Locations of jobs: United States and some international
Frequency of updates: Daily
Search by: Job category; Keyword; Level of experience; Job type; Location
Resume database available: Yes
Employer profiles available: Yes
Costs for job seekers: Free

Costs for employers: $125 per posting each month, or $695 per month for unlimited postings.

Other key features: Job Hunter e-zine offering career advice; instructional job search videos; and interview, salary, and negotiation links.

Comments: Geared toward recent college graduates, this site is a step-by-step guide to getting a job, with everything from resume preparation to interviewing tips to negotiating an employment offer. Many major employers detail their internship programs here. There are also links to a variety of other job hunting Web sites. A solid choice for those new to the job market, the site includes opportunities for recent grads with experience.

COLLEGE NEWS

www.collegenews.com
Number of job listings: Over 250
Types of jobs: Entry-level; Internships; Summer; Temporary
Locations of jobs: United States
Frequency of updates: Monthly
Search by: Job category
Resume database available: Yes
Costs for job seekers: Free
Costs for employers: Contact site
Other key features: Extensive information relating to student life and college and career planning.
Comments: Not as many job listings here as other places, but the additional features this site has to offer makes it an interesting stop for college job seekers.

COOL WORKS

www.coolworks.com
Number of job listings: 75,000
Types of jobs: Seasonal employment at national parks, resorts, and camps
Locations of jobs: United States
Frequency of updates:
Search by: Company name; Job category; Job environment; Location
Resume database available: Yes
Employer profiles available: Yes
Costs for job seekers: Free

Costs for employers: $75 per month for seasonal and career positions, or $75 for a "Help Wanted Now!" posting for seven days.

Other key features: Cool links; the Cool Works Community; weekly e-updates; and "links we like."

Comments: Cool Works does a good job of covering a unique market. Job seekers can look at opportunities at famous national parks, amusement parks, ski resorts, and more.

GRADUATING ENGINEER & COMPUTER CAREERS

www.careertech.com

Number of job listings: Less than 250

Types of jobs: Entry-level engineering and high-tech positions

Locations of jobs: United States

Frequency of updates:

Search by: Location; College major

Resume database available: Yes

Employer profiles available: Yes

Costs for job seekers: Free

Costs for employers: $100 for a 30-day posting

Other key features: Profiles of engineering and high-tech careers; "fun" companies; and high-tech companies; information on salary expectations; regional information; and general information concerning relative industries.

Comments: Registration is required to use this site.

MONSTERTRAK.COM

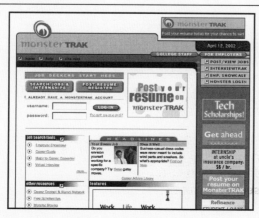

www.jobtrak.com
Types of jobs: All
Locations of jobs: United States
Frequency of updates: Daily
Search by: School; Job type; Job category; Location; Keyword
Resume database available: Yes
Employer profiles available: Yes
Costs for job seekers: Free
Costs for employers: Ranges from $25 for a single listing targeting one campus, to $395 for the listing to be open to all of the over 1,200 colleges.
Other key features: Scholarship search; career guide; alumni network; relocation information; major-to-career converter, and more.
Comments: Geared directly toward college students, MBAs, and alumni through college career centers, MonsterTrak.com has partnerships with more than 1,200 campuses and Monster.com.

RISING STAR INTERNSHIPS

www.rsinternships.com
Number of job listings: Under 1,000
Types of jobs: Internships
Locations of jobs: United States and some international
Frequency of updates: Daily
Search by: Industry
Resume database available: Yes
Employer profiles available: Yes
Costs for job seekers: Free

Costs for employers: $10 per month for continuous recruiting, or $20 for a single month, $50 for three months, $85 for six months, or $150 for a year.

Other key features: List of colleges, universities, technical schools, and graduate schools with links to the schools' Web sites.

Comments: This site provides listings of internship opportunities only, and provides good coverage of industries, though not being able to select specific locations is a nuisance.

SNAGAJOB.COM

www.snagajob.com

Types of jobs: Part-time and seasonal

Locations of jobs: United States

Frequency of updates: As submitted

Search by: Job category; Location

Resume database available: Yes (in the form of an online application system)

Employer profiles available: Yes

Costs for job seekers: Free

Costs for employers: $89 per job posting

Other key features: Articles targeting college and high-school students; resume and interview tips; and student employment regulation information.

Comments: SnagAJob.com provides a lot of good information for first-time job seekers in addition to the job listings. This is one of the few sites that also caters to high-school students.

SUMMERJOBS.COM

www.summerjobs.com

Number of job listings: Over 250

Types of jobs: Summer jobs

Locations of jobs: United States and some international

Frequency of updates: As submitted

Search by: Keyword; Location

Resume database available: Yes

Employer profiles available: Yes

Costs for job seekers: Free

Costs for employers: Starts at $42 for four weeks; at the time of this writing, they were also offering a free one-week job posting for new users.

Other key features: Electronic newsletters for job seekers and employers; links to other job search sites; and "hot topics" articles.

Search Engines

Another way to find job listings on the Web is to perform a keyword search in a search engine such as Yahoo! or Lycos. Try using keywords like "employment opportunities," "job listings," or "positions available." Some of the most popular search engines include:

AltaVista
www.altavista.com

Infoseek
www.infoseek.com

byteSearch
www.bytesearch.com

Lycos
www.lycos.com

Direct Hit
www.directhit.com

Mamma.com
www.mamma.com

Excite
www.excite.com

Northern Light
www.northernlight.com

Go Network
www.go.com

OneBlink
www.oneblink.com

Google
www.google.com

Snap
www.snap.com

GoTo.com
www.goto.com

WebCrawler
www.webcrawler.com

HotBot
www.hotbot.com

Yahoo!
www.yahoo.com

There are many more search engines available, offering various search capabilities, from Web-wide searches to geographically specific searches. We suggest focusing first on the Web sites listed in this chapter, and then utilize a search engine if you need to find more information.

CHAPTER FOUR

SEARCHING FOR JOBS BY GEOGRAPHIC AREA

The most traditional job search, of course, involves rushing out to get the local paper on Sunday morning, and then circling ads in the Help Wanted section. Thanks to the Internet, you don't have to wait until Sunday anymore, and you won't need to plunk down the cost of the newspaper, either. Best of all, your job search needn't be limited to just those newspapers easily available where you live. The newspaper and other local and regional Web sites in this chapter will enable you to search job listings specific to just about any area of the United States, as well as jobs in a number of other countries.

Even if you are limiting your job search to one city or region, be sure to also take advantage of the resources discussed in other chapters of this book. Many of the general job sites listed in Chapter Three have search capabilities that enable you to look for jobs in a particular city, state, or area. For example, America's Job Bank (**www.ajb.org**), a site with more than one million job listings, has a helpful feature that allows you to limit your job title or keyword searches to jobs within various ranges of 5 to 100 miles away from a particular zip code.

In Chapter Five, many of the sites for specific industries will have similar search capabilities. In addition, some of the industries presented are largely concentrated in a particular city or area. Many of the government jobs at Federal Jobs Central (**www.fedjobs.com**), for example, will be based around Washington, D.C., while the media and publishing positions posted at MediaBistro (**www.mediabistro.com**) will often be in New York City (though other areas are also well represented). The important thing to remember is that for a thorough and successful-job search, you should seek out all available jobs through a variety of local, national, and industry-specific sources.

U.S. Job Sites by Region and State
Northeast/Mid-Atlantic
Area newspapers with online classifieds:

CONNECTICUT

Connecticut Post
www.connpost.com

Fairfield County Weekly
www.fairfieldweekly.com

Greenwich Time
www.greenwichtime.com

Hartford Advocate
www.hartfordadvocate.com

Hartford Courant
www.hartfordcourant.com

Meriden Record-Journal
www.record-journal.com

New Haven Advocate
www.newhavenadvocate.com

New Haven Register
www.newhavenregister.com

New London Day
www.theday.com

The News-Times (Danbury)
www.newstimes.com

Stamford Advocate
www.stamfordadvocate.com

Stratford Bard
www.stratfordbard.com

DELAWARE

Cape Gazette (Rehoboth Beach)
www.capegazette.com

Dover Post
www.doverpost.com

The Newark Post
www.ncbl.com/post

The Newcastle Business Ledger
www.ncbl.com

The News Journal
www.delawareonline.com

MAINE

Bangor Daily News
www.bangornews.com

Kennebec Journal (Augusta)
www.kjonline.com

Lewiston Sun Journal
www.sunjournal.com

Portland Press Herald
www.portland.com

MASSACHUSETTS

The Boston Globe
www.boston.com

The Enterprise (Brockton)
www.enterprisenews.com

The Boston Herald
www.bostonherald.com

The Boston Phoenix
www.bostonphoenix.com

Cape Cod Times
www.capecodtimes.com

Daily Hampshire Gazette
(Northampton)
www.gazettenet.com

The Eagle-Tribune (Lawrence)
www.eagletribune.com

The Herald News (Fall River)
www.heraldnews.com

The Patriot Ledger (Quincy)
www.southofboston.com

The Springfield Union News
www.masslive.com

The Standard-Times
(New Bedford)
www.s-t.com

Worcester Telegram & Gazette
www.telegram.com

NEW HAMPSHIRE

Concord Monitor
www.cmonitor.com

Nashua Telegraph
www.nashuatelegraph.com

Portsmouth Herald
www.seacoastonline.com

The Union Leader (Manchester)
www.theunionleader.com

NEW JERSEY

Ashbury Park Press
www.injersey.com

Courier-Post (Camden)
www.courierpostonline.com

Home News Tribune (East Brunswick)
www.thnt.com

The Press of Atlantic City
www.pressplus.com

The Princeton Packet
www.packetonline.com

The Record (Bergen-Hackensack)
www.bergen.com

The Star-Ledger (Newark)
www.nj.com/starledger

The Times (Trenton)
www.nj.com/times

NEW YORK

The Buffalo News
www.buffalonews.com

The Daily Gazette (Schenectady)
www.dailygazette.com

The Journal News (White Plains)
www.nyjournalnews.com

Long Island Newsday
www.newsday.com

The New York Times
www.nytimes.com

Observer-Dispatch (Utica)
www.uticaod.com

The Press & Sun Bulletin (Binghamton)
www.pressconnects.com

Rochester Democrat & Chronicle
www.rochesternews.com

New York Daily News
www.nydailynews.com

New York Post
www.nypostonline.com

Syracuse Herald-Journal
www.syracuse.com

Times Union (Albany)
www.timesunion.com

PENNSYLVANIA

Centre Daily Times (State College)
www.centredaily.com

The Citizens' Voice (Wilkes-Barre)
www.citizensvoice.com

The Inquirer (Philadelphia)
www.philly.com

Intelligencer Journal (Lancaster)
www.lancnews.com

The Morning Call (Allentown)
www.mcall.com

Philadelphia Daily News
www.philly.com/mld/dailynews

Pittsburgh Post-Gazette
www.post-gazette.com

Reading Eagle & Reading Times
www.readingeagle.com

The Scranton Times
www.scrantontimes.com

The Tribune Review (Pittsburgh)
www.tribune-review.com

The York Dispatch
www.yorkdispatch.com

RHODE ISLAND

Bristol Phoenix
www.bristolri.com

The Call (Woonsocket)
www.woonsocketcall.com

The Pawtucket Times
www.pawtuckettimes.com

The Providence Journal
www.projo.com

VERMONT

The Burlington Free Press
www.burlingtonfreepress.com

The Caledonian-Record (St. Johnsbury)
www.caledonian-record.com

The Rutland Herald
www.rutlandherald.com

Times Argus (Barre)
www.timesargus.com

BOSTONHIRE.COM

www.bostonhire.com
Number of job listings: Over 250
Types of jobs: All
Locations of jobs: Boston metropolitan area
Frequency of updates: Daily

Search by: Job category; Keyword
Resume database available: Yes
Employer profiles available: Yes
Costs for job seekers: Free
Costs for employers: $95 per ad running 60 days, or $75 per ad for three or more job postings. Bulk rates and comprehensive memberships that include resume access are also available.
Other key features: Includes a schedule of Massachusetts job fairs and a series of articles related to a job search.

BOSTON JOB BANK

www.bostonjobs.com
Number of job listings: Over 250
Types of jobs: All
Locations of jobs: Boston metropolitan area
Frequency of updates: Daily
Search by: Job category; Keyword
Resume database available: Yes
Employer profiles available: No
Costs for job seekers: Free
Costs for employers: $35 per ad for two months. Resume access is free.
Comments: A simple, no-frills career site providing current, thorough information. A number of freelance and part-time positions were also posted. A drawback is the limited number of job categories from which you can choose (professional, computer, business, sales, general).

BostonSearch

www.bostonsearch.com

Number of job listings: Fewer than 1,000

Types of jobs: All

Locations of jobs: Boston metropolitan area

Frequency of updates: Daily

Search by: Job category; Job type; Keyword

Resume database available: Yes

Employer profiles available: Yes

Costs for job seekers: Free

Costs for employers: Start at $85 per ad running 45 days. Membership packages and research services are also available. Contact site for details.

Other key features: Weekly career advice column; job search agent; hints and tips; an online bookstore; several special research categories (real estate, sports, etc.); and links to current news.

Comments: A nice feature of this site is that most searches performed will put all of the results on a single page.

Capital Area Help Wanted

www.capitalareahelpwanted.com

Number of job listings: Over 250

Types of jobs: All

Locations of jobs: New York Capital Region

Frequency of updates: Daily

Search by: Job category; Location; Job title; Keyword; Company name

Resume database available: Yes

Employer profiles available: No
Costs for job seekers: Free
Costs for employers: $198 for 30 days
Other key features: Job search agent; job seeker FAQ; and links to resume services.
Comments: This site is part of the Regional Help Wanted network.

DELAWARE, STATE OF

www.delawarepersonnel.com/empserv/jobs/search.htm
Types of jobs: All, primarily government
Locations of jobs: Delaware
Frequency of updates: Weekly
Search by: Department; Keyword; Salary; Date posted
Resume database available: No
Employer profiles available: No
Costs for job seekers: Free
Comments: This site is a service of the Delaware State Personnel Office and maintains links to information about their services, and contact information including a phone directory, online feedback form, and a listing of office locations.

JOBNET

www.jobnet.com
Number of job listings: Over 250
Types of jobs: All
Locations of jobs: Philadelphia metropolitan area
Frequency of updates: Daily
Search by: Job category; Keyword; Location; Date posted
Resume database available: Yes
Employer profiles available: No
Costs for job seekers: Free
Costs for employers: For nonmembers, the cost is $95 per ad running 30 days. Memberships and bulk posting package deals are also available. Contact site for more information.
Other key features: Offers the "Jobnet Works!" service, which allows employers and recruiters to create a functional jobs section on their own Web sites.
Comments: This is one of the few job sites that seems to offer more to employers than job seekers.

NJ Jobs

www.njjobs.com
Number of job listings: Over 250
Types of jobs: All
Locations of jobs: New Jersey
Frequency of updates: Weekly
Search by: Keyword
Resume database available: Yes
Employer profiles available: No
Costs for job seekers: Free
Costs for employers: $25 per ad per week. First-time advertisers can place an ad for free for one week, with a restriction of two ads per weekly listing.
Other key features: Links to New Jersey-related sites and events.
Comments: The quality of the job listings was a bit surprising, considering the no-frills layout and function of the site. Many went into great detail about the available positions and companies looking for job candidates.

Philadelphia Online

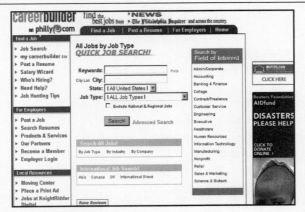

http://careers.philly.com
Types of jobs: All
Locations of jobs: Philadelphia metropolitan area
Frequency of updates: Daily
Search by: Job category; Keyword; Location
Resume database available: Yes
Employer profiles available: Yes

Costs for job seekers: Free

Costs for employers: $200 per job for 30 days. For an additional $50, ads can be cross-posted on other job sites.

Other key features: Salary wizard; career trivia; articles; and a series of local resources, including job fair information, ask the experts, and a career resource center.

Comments: This site is part of the CareerBuilder Network.

SOUTHOFBOSTON.COM

www.southofboston.com
Number of job listings: Over 1,000
Types of jobs: All
Locations of jobs: Southeastern Massachusetts
Frequency of updates: Daily
Search by: Date posted; Keyword; Job category; Location
Resume database available: No
Employer profiles available: No
Costs for job seekers: Free
Costs for employers: Rates are based upon ad type, size, and the print versions in which the ad will also appear. Contact site for complete details.
Other key features: Ad Alert e-mail notification service.
Comments: SouthOfBoston.com is an online version of the classifieds of 12 South Shore and southeastern Massachusetts newspapers.

VERMONT DEPARTMENT OF EMPLOYMENT AND TRAINING

www.det.state.vt.us
Number of job listings: Over 1,000
Types of jobs: All
Locations of jobs: Vermont (also has access to nationwide listings)
Frequency of updates: Daily
Search by: Date posted; Education; Job category; Job type; Keyword; Location; Experience
Resume database available: Yes
Employer profiles available: No
Costs for job seekers: Free
Costs for employers: Free to Vermont employers

Other key features: Offers access to Vermont labor market information, unemployment rates, statewide wages, and employment statistics; a summer jobs section; access to Federal and national job listings; and links to additional job listings and training programs.

Comments: Job seekers registered with this site may request that a referral be sent from the Vermont Department of Employment and Training directly to an employer. Large-scope searches tend to take awhile; however, the lists generated include such highly useful information as experience requirements, salary, job title, and location.

Southeast

Area newspapers with online classifieds:

ALABAMA

The Andalusia Star News
www.andalusiastarnews.com

Anniston Star
www.annistonstar.com

Birmingham News
www.al.com/birmingham

Birmingham Post-Herald
www.postherald.com

Daily Mountain Eagle (Jasper)
www.mountaineagle.com

Decatur Daily
www.decaturdaily.com

The Gadsen Times
www.gadsentimes.com

Huntsville Times
www.al.com/huntsville

Mobile Register
www.al.com/mobile

Montgomery Advertiser
www.montgomeryadvertiser.com

The Times-Journal (Fort Payne)
www.times-journal.com

Troy Messenger
www.troymessenger.com

ARKANSAS

Arkansas Democrat-Gazette
www.ardemgaz.com

Arkansas Employment Register
www.arjobs.com

Batesville Daily Guard
www.guardonline.com

The Benton Courier
www.bentoncourier.com

The Daily Citizen (Searcy)
www.thedailycitizen.com

Harrison Daily Times
www.harrisondailytimes.com

Hope Star
www.hopestar.com

Jonesboro Sun
www.jonesborosun.com

Morning News of Northwest Arkansas
www.nwamorningnews.com

Newport Daily Independent
www.newportindependent.com

El Dorado News-Times
www.eldoradonews.com

Northwest Arkansas Times
www.nwarktimes.com

The Glenwood Democrat
www.glenwooddemocrat.com

The Sentinel-Record (Hot Springs)
sentinel.townnews.com

DISTRICT OF COLUMBIA

Roll Call
www.rollcall.com

Washington Post
www.washingtonpost.com

Washington City Paper
www.washingtoncitypaper.com

The Washington Times
www.washtimes.com

FLORIDA

Bradenton Herald
www.bradentonherald.com

The News-Press (Fort Myers)
www.news-press.com

The Florida Times-Union (Jacksonville)
www.jacksonville.com

Northwest Florida Daily News
www.nwfdailynews.com

Florida Today (Melbourne)
www.flatoday.com

Orlando Sentinel
www.orlandosentinel.com

Gainesville Sun
www.sunone.com

Pensacola News Journal
www.pensacolanewsjournal.com

Herald-Tribune Newscoast (Sarasota)
www.newscoast.com

St. Petersburg Times
www.sptimes.com

The Miami Herald
www.herald.com

The Sun-Sentinel (Fort Lauderdale)
www.sun-sentinel.com

Naples Daily News
www.naplesnews.com

Tallahassee Democrat
www.tdo.com

The News Herald (Panama City)
www.newsherald.com

Tampa Tribune
www.tampatrib.com

GEORGIA

The Albany Herald
www.albanyherald.com

LaGrange Daily News
www.lagrangenews.com

Athens Banner-Herald
www.onlineathens.com

Ledger Enquirer (Columbus)
www.l-e-o.com

Atlanta Daily World
www.atlantadailyworld.com

Macon Telegraph
www.macontel.com

The Atlanta Journal-Constitution
www.ajc.com

Rockdale Citizen
www.rockdalecitizen.com

The Augusta Chronicle
www.augustachronicle.com

Savannah Morning News
www.savannahnow.com

The Courier-Herald (Dublin)
www.courier-herald.com

Waycross Journal-Herald
www.wjhnews.com

KENTUCKY

The Courier-Journal (Louisville)
www.courier-journal.com

LOUISIANA

The Advocate (Baton Rouge)
www.theadvocate.com

New Orleans City Business
http://citybusiness.neworleans.com

The Daily World (Lafayette)
www.dailyworld.com

The Times (Natchitoches)
www.nwlouisiana.com

Houma Today
www.houmatoday.com

Times-Picayune (New Orleans)
www.nola.com

MARYLAND

The Baltimore Sun
www.sunspot.net

The Daily Record (Baltimore)
www.mddailyrecord.com

The Capital (Annapolis)
www.hometownannapolis.com

The Frederick News-Post
www.fredericknewspost.com

Cumberland Times-News
www.times-news.com

The Herald-Mail (Hagerstown)
www.herald-mail.com

MISSISSIPPI

The Clarion-Ledger (Jackson)
www.clarionledger.com

Northeast Mississippi Daily Journal
www.djournal.com/djournal/site

Enterprise-Journal (McComb)
www.enterprise-journal.com

The Oxford Eagle
www.oxfordeagle.com

The Natchez Democrat
www.natchezdemocrat.com

The Sun Herald (Biloxi)
www.sunherald.com

NORTH CAROLINA

Asheville Citizen-Times
www.citizen-times.com

The News & Observer (Raleigh)
www.news-observer.com

The Charlotte Observer
www.charlotte.com

The News & Record (Greensboro)
www.thedepot.com

Fayetteville Observer
www.fayettevillenc.com

The Sampson Independent
www.clintonnc.com

The Herald-Sun (Durham)
www.herald-sun.com

The Winston-Salem Journal
www.journalnow.com

SOUTH CAROLINA

The Greenville News
www.greenvilleonline.com

The Spartanburg Herald-Journal
www.goupstate.com

The Post and Courier (Charleston)
www.charleston.net

The State (Columbia)
www.thestate.com

TENNESSEE

The Commercial Appeal (Memphis)
www.gomemphis.com

The Knoxville News-Sentinel
www.knoxnews.com

The Jackson Sun
www.jacksonsun.com

The Tennessean (Nashville)
www.tennessean.com

VIRGINIA

The Alexandria Journal
www.jrnl.com

The Montgomery Journal
www.jrnl.com

The Arlington Journal
www.jrnl.com

The Roanoke Times
www.roanoke.com

The Daily Press (Newport News)
www.dailypress.com

Virginian-Pilot (Norfolk)
www.pilotonline.com

The Daily Progress (Charlottesville)
www.dailyprogress.com

Richmond Times-Dispatch
www.gatewayva.com

WEST VIRGINIA

Charleston Daily Mail
www.dailymail.com

The Herald-Dispatch (Huntington)
www.hdonline.com

The Charleston Gazette
www.wvgazette.com

The Intelligencer (Wheeling)
www.theintelligencer.net

The Dominion Post
www.dominionpost.com

The Register-Herald (Beckley)
www.register-herald.com

ALEX (Automated Labor Exchange system)

www.alex.vec.state.va.us
Number of job listings: Over 30,000
Types of jobs: All
Locations of jobs: Primarily Virginia
Frequency of updates: Daily
Search by: Job category; Keyword; Location; Military occupation code
Resume database available: No
Employer profiles available: No
Costs for job seekers: Free
Costs for employers: Free
Comments: This site is a service of the Virginia Employment Commission.

Florida CareerLink

www.floridacareerlink.com
Number of job listings: Over 250
Types of jobs: All
Locations of jobs: Florida
Frequency of updates: Daily
Search by: Job category; Location; Keyword
Resume database available: No
Employer profiles available: Yes
Costs for job seekers: Free
Costs for employers: $295 for a six-week posting. Additional options and discounts available.

Other key features: Information on local career fairs; relocation information; job search advice; diversity and college links; stress relief; and links to recruiters and other career sites.

Comments: Job listings are current and fairly well detailed.

THINKJOBS.COM

www.thinkjobs.com
Number of job listings: Over 800
Types of jobs: Technical and Energy
Locations of jobs: Southeastern United States
Frequency of updates: Daily
Search by: Keyword; Job type; Salary; Location; Job title
Resume database available: Yes
Employer profiles available: No
Costs for job seekers: Free
Costs for employers: Fees are based on an hourly rate. Contact site for complete details.
Other key features: Resume broadcaster; job search agent; and links to other job search sites.
Comments: This is a great site for people interested in technical jobs, especially since it covers the entire southeastern region of the United States rather than just a single city or state.

TRIANGLE JOBS

www.trianglejobs.com
Number of job listings: Over 1,500
Types of jobs: All
Locations of jobs: North and South Carolina

Frequency of updates:

Search by: Date posted; Job category; Job title; Type of ad; Publication

Resume database available: Yes

Employer profiles available: Yes

Costs for job seekers: Free

Costs for employers: $215 for 30 days online; includes a free five-line ad in the Sunday classified section.

Other key features: Job fair information; salary calculator; and a job search agent.

Comments: An ideal site for a job seeker wishing to relocate to the Carolinas.

Midwest

Area newspapers with online classifieds:

ILLINOIS

The Beacon News
www.suburbanchicagonews.com

The Benton Evening News
www.bentoneveningnews.com

Canton Daily Ledger
http://canton.townnews.com

Chicago Sun-Times
www.suntimes.com

Chicago Tribune
www.chicagotribune.com

Crain's Chicago Business
www.crainschicagobusiness.com

The Daily Clay County Advocate-Press
www.advocatepress.com

Daily Herald (Arlington Heights)
www.dailyherald.com

Daily Southtown (Chicago)
www.dailysouthtown.com

The Dispatch (Moline)
www.qconline.com

Herald & Review (Decatur)
www.herald-review.com

The Morning Sentinel (Centralia)
www.morningsentinel.com

The News-Gazette (Champaign-Urbana)
www.news-gazette.com

Northwest Herald (Crystal Lake)
www.nwherald.com

Peoria Journal Star
www.pjstar.com

The Rockford Register Star
www.rrstar.com

The Rock Island Argus
www.qconline.com

Southern Illinoisan
www.southernillinoisan.com

The State Journal-Register (Springfield)
www.sj-r.com

The Telegraph (Alton)
www.thetelegraph.com

INDIANA

The Bloomington Independent
www.indepen.com

The Indianapolis Star
www.starnews.com

Evansville Courier & Press
www.courierpress.com

The Journal Gazette (Fort Wayne)
http://web.journalgazette.net

Fort Wayne News-Sentinel
http://web.news-sentinel.com

Nuvo Newsweekly (Indianapolis)
www.nuvo.net

The Goshen News
www.goshennews.com

The Post-Tribune (Gary)
www.post-trib.com

The Hammond Times
www.thetimesonline.com

South Bend Tribune
www.southbendtribune.com

The Herald Press (Huntington)
www.h-ponline.com

The Star Press (Muncie)
www.thestarpress.com

The Herald Times (Bloomington)
www.hoosiertimes.com

The Tribune-Star (Terre Haute)
www.tribstar.com

IOWA

The Des Moines Register
www.dmregister.com

The Sioux City Journal
www.siouxcityjournal.com

The Gazette (Cedar Rapids)
www.gazetteonline.com

The Telegraph Herald (Dubuque)
www.thonline.com

The Iowa City Press-Citizen
www.press-citizen.com

The Waterloo-Cedar Falls Courier
www.wcfcourier.com

KANSAS

Kansas City Kansan
www.kansascitykansan.com

The Salina Journal
www.saljournal.com

Lawrence Journal-World
www.ljworld.com

The Topeka Capital-Journal
www.cjonline.com

The Olathe Daily News
www.olathedailynews.com

The Wichita Eagle
www.wichitaeagle.com

MICHIGAN

The Ann Arbor News
http://aa.mlive.com

The Grand Rapids Press
http://gr.mlive.com

Crain's Detroit Business
www.crainsdetroit.com

The Detroit Free Press
www.freep.com

The Detroit News
www.detnews.com

The Flint Journal
http://fl.mlive.com

The Kalamazoo Gazette
http://kz.mlive.com

Lansing State Journal
www.lansingstatejournal.com

Metro Times (Detroit)
www.metrotimes.com

The Muskegon Chronicle
http://mu.mlive.com

MINNESOTA

Duluth News Tribune
www.duluthnews.com

The Independent (Marshall)
www.marshallindependent.com

Post-Bulletin (Rochester)
www.postbulletin.com

St. Cloud Times
www.sctimes.com

St. Paul Pioneer Press
www.pioneerplanet.com

Star Tribune (Minneapolis-St. Paul)
www.startribune.com

MISSOURI

Columbia Missourian
www.digmo.org

The Examiner (Independence)
www.examiner.net

The Joplin Globe
www.joplinglobe.com

The Kansas City Star
www.kcstar.com

St. Joseph News-Press
www.stjoenews-press.com

St. Louis Post-Dispatch
www.postnet.com

The St. Louis Suburban Journals
www.stltoday.com

The Springfield News-Leader
www.springfieldnews-leader.com

NEBRASKA

Lincoln Journal Star
www.journalstar.com

Omaha World Herald
www.omaha.com

The North Platte Telegraph
www.nptelegraph.com

Scottsbluff Star-Herald
www.starherald.com

NORTH DAKOTA

Bismarck Tribune
www.bismarcktribune.com

The Forum (Fargo)
www.in-forum.com

Grand Forks Herald
www.gfherald.com

Minot Daily News
www.ndweb.com/mdnonline

OHIO

The Beacon Journal (Akron)
www.ohio.com/bj

The Columbus Dispatch
www.dispatch.com

The Blade (Toledo)
www.toledoblade.com

Journal-News (Hamilton)
www.journal-news.com

The Canton Repository
www.cantonrep.com

The Plain Dealer (Cleveland)
www.cleveland.com

The Cincinnati Enquirer
www.enquirer.com

Sandusky Register
www.sanduskyregister.com

The Cincinnati Post
www.cincypost.com

Tribune Chronicle (Warren)
www.tribunechronicle.com

SOUTH DAKOTA

Aberdeen American News
www.aberdeennews.com

Huron Plainsman
www.plainsman.com

Argus Leader
www.argusleader.com

Pierre Capital Journal
www.capjournal.com

WISCONSIN

The Capital Times (Madison)
www.madison.com

Kenosha News
www.kenoshacounty.com

Eau Claire Leader Telegram
www.leadertelegram.com

Marshfield News-Herald
www.marshfieldnewsherald.com

The Green Bay News-Chronicle
www.greenbaynewschron.com

Milwaukee Journal Sentinel
www.jsonline.com

Green Bay Press-Gazette
www.greenbaypressgazette.com

The Northwestern
www.thenorthwestern.com

The Journal Times (Racine)
www.racinecounty.com

Wisconsin State Journal (Madison)
www.madison.com

CAREERBOARD.COM

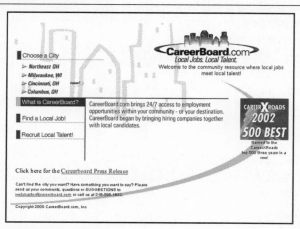

www.careerboard.com

Types of jobs: All

Locations of jobs: The Akron, Cincinnati, Cleveland, Columbus, and Milwaukee metropolitan areas

Frequency of updates: Daily

Search by: Date posted; Job category; Job type; Keyword

Resume database available: Yes

Employer profiles available: Yes

Costs for job seekers: Free

Costs for employers: Vary depending on which region you choose. Rates are available for a single posting, a profile page, a five-pack of posting credits, a ten-pack of posting credits, and monthly and annual membership packages.

Other key features: Job search agent; free newsletter for employers; and area guides for each of the regions.

Comments: Job listings include company and benefits information and links to the company's Web site.

CAREER CONNECTOR

www.careerconnector.com

Number of job listings: Over 15,000

Types of jobs: All

Locations of jobs: Chicago metropolitan area

Frequency of updates: Daily

Search by: Date posted; Job category; Keyword; Location; Salary

Resume database available: Yes
Employer profiles available: No
Costs for job seekers: Free
Costs for employers: Free
Other key features: Job seekers can view the most recently posted job openings; separate listings for internships/co-ops; job search agents; and general information on various apprenticeships.

CAREERLINK.ORG

www.careerlink.org
Number of job listings: Over 1,000
Types of jobs: All
Locations of jobs: Nebraska
Frequency of updates: Daily
Search by: Job category; Job title
Resume database available: Yes
Employer profiles available: Yes
Costs for job seekers: Free
Costs for employers: Listings start at $150 per ad. Many membership packages that include unlimited postings, corporate profiles, and resume access are also available.
Other key features: Detailed employer profiles and job descriptions; company listings are also broken down by community and industry.
Comments: This is an impressive site, and one of the few sites you will find devoted to employment in Nebraska. This site is operated by the Applied Information Management Institute, and is a member of the whohasjobs.com network.

KANSASJOBS.COM

www.kansasjobs.com
Number of job listings: Under 250
Types of jobs: All
Locations of jobs: Kansas
Frequency of updates: As submitted
Search by: Location
Resume database available: Yes
Employer profiles available: Yes
Costs for job seekers: Free
Costs for employers: Rates start at $150 for a single job posting and company profile. Other packages are available. Contact site for more information.
Other key features: Links to recruiters and colleges in Kansas; resume blaster; and resume and cover letter hints and tips.
Comments: This site does not appear to be run by the Kansas Department of Human Resources, which explains why far fewer job listings are available and the cost for employers has risen since our last review.

MINNESOTAJOBS.COM

www.minnesotajobs.com
Types of jobs: All
Locations of jobs: Minnesota
Frequency of updates: Daily
Search by: Job category; Keyword
Resume database available: Yes
Employer profiles available: Yes

Costs for job seekers: Free
Costs for employers: $60 per month
Other key features: Newsletters; recruiting tips; links to Minnesota associations; salary surveys; job fairs; and articles.
Comments: While the site's functions work fairly well, the busy layout and neon color scheme are a bit hard on the eyes, making the site difficult to read at times.

MISSOURI, STATE OF

www.oa.state.mo.us/stjobs.htm
Types of jobs: State job opportunities
Locations of jobs: Missouri
Frequency of updates: As submitted
Search by: Department
Resume database available: No
Employer profiles available: No
Costs for job seekers: Free
Other key features: Each department has links to information relevant to the department's purpose.
Comments: This site is essentially a directory pointing to available positions within various departments and agencies in the Missouri state government.

ONLINE COLUMBIA

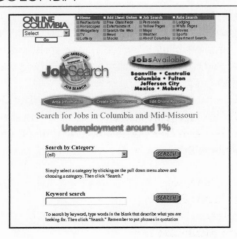

www.onlinecolumbia.com/jobsearch.asp
Number of job listings: Under 250
Types of jobs: All
Locations of jobs: Mid-Missouri
Frequency of updates: Daily
Search by: Keyword; Job category
Resume database available: Yes
Employer profiles available: No
Costs for job seekers: Free
Costs for employers: Contact site
Other key features: Contains links of interest to people moving to or visiting the mid-Missouri area.
Comments: The links to company Web sites within the ads are a handy feature.

WISCONSIN EMPLOYMENT CONNECTION

www.dwd.state.wi.us/jobnet
Types of jobs: All
Locations of jobs: Wisconsin, Iowa, Minnesota, Northern Illinois, Michigan
Frequency of updates: As submitted
Search by: Company name; Job category; Job title; Location
Resume database available: No
Employer profiles available: Yes (as part of ad)
Costs for job seekers: Free
Costs for employers: Free
Other key features: Quarterly newsletter; job description writer for employers; employability checkup; job search and resume advice. Another nice feature is that any job listing close to public transportation has a bus icon next to it.
Comments: Operated by the State of Wisconsin Department of Workforce Development, this site runs off the "more is better" philosophy. The search criteria make it difficult to narrow your search down, making the jobs list full of multiple useless listings.

West/Southwest

Area newspapers with online classifieds:

ALASKA

Anchorage Daily News
www.adn.com

The Anchorage Press
www.anchoragepress.com

Eagle Eye Journal (Haines)
www.eagleyenews.com

Fairbanks Daily News-Miner
www.newsminer.com

Frontiersman (Wasilla)
www.frontiersman.com

Juneau Empire
www.juneauempire.com

ARIZONA

Arizona Daily Star (Tucson)
www.azstarnet.com

Arizona Daily Sun (Flagstaff)
www.azdailysun.com

Arizona Republic (Phoenix)
www.arizonarepublic.com

The Daily Courier (Prescott)
www.prescottaz.com

Mohave Valley News (Bullhead City)
www.mohavedailynews.com

Today's News-Herald
www.havasunews.com

Tucson Citizen
www.tucsoncitizen.com

The Yuma Daily Sun
www.yumasun.com

CALIFORNIA

Antelope Valley Press (Palmdale)
www.avpress.com

Auburn Journal
www.auburnjournal.com

The Bakersfield Californian
www.bakersfield.com

The Californian (Salinas)
www.thecalifornian.com

Chico Enterprise Record
www.chicoer.com

Contra Costa Times
www.hotcoco.com

Daily News Los Angeles
www.dailynews.com

Los Angeles Times
www.latimes.com

Marin Independent Journal
www.marinij.com

Merced Sun-Star
www.mercedsun-star.com

Modesto Bee
www.modbee.com

Napa Valley Register
www.napanews.com

North County Times
www.nctimes.net

Orange County Register
www.ocregister.com

Daily Republic (Fairfield)
www.dailyrepublic.com

The Daily Triplicate (Crescent City)
www.triplicate.com

The Davis Enterprise
www.davisenterprise.com

The Desert Sun (Palm Springs)
www.thedesertsun.com

Fresno Bee
www.fresnobee.com

Huntington Beach News
hb.quik.com/jperson/

The Lodi News-Sentinel
www.lodinews.com

Long Beach Press-Telegram
www.press-telegram.com

The Press Enterprise (Riverside)
www.pe.com

Sacramento Bee
www.sacbee.com

San Bernadino County Sun
www.sbcsun.com

San Diego Union-Tribune
www.uniontrib.com

San Francisco Chronicle
www.sfgate.com/chronicle

San Francisco Examiner
www.examiner.com

San Jose Mercury News
www.bayarea.com

Santa Barbara News-Press
www.newspress.com

COLORADO

Aspen Daily News
www.aspendailynews.com

Boulder Daily Camera
www.thedailycamera.com

Broomfield News
www.broomfieldnews.com

Denver Post
www.denverpost.com

Durango Herald
www.durangoherald.com

The Gazette (Colorado Springs)
www.gazette.com

Grand Junction Sentinel
www.gjsentinel.com

The Greeley Daily Tribune
www.greeleytrib.com

Montrose Daily Press
www.montrosepress.com

The Pueblo Chieftain
www.chieftain.com

Rocky Mountain News (Denver)
www.insidedenver.com

Summit Daily News
www.summitdaily.com

Telluride Daily Planet
www.telluridegateway.com

Vail Daily
www.vaildaily.com

HAWAII

The Garden Island (Lihue)
www.kauaiworld.com

Lahaina News
www.westmaui.com

Hawaii Tribune-Herald
www.hilohawaiitribune.com

Maui News
www.mauinews.com

Honolulu Star-Bulletin
www.starbulletin.com

West Hawaii Today
www.westhawaiitoday.com

IDAHO

The Challis Messenger
www.challismessenger.com

Idaho State Journal (Pocatello)
www.journalnet.com

The Coeur d'Alene Press
www.cdapress.com

Idaho Statesman (Boise)
www.idahostatesman.com

Idaho Press-Tribune (Nampa)
www.idahopress.com

Post Register (Idaho Falls)
www.idahonews.com

MONTANA

Billings Gazette
www.billingsgazette.com

The Missoulian
www.missoulian.com

Bozeman Daily Chronicle
www.gomontana.com

The Montana Standard (Butte)
www.mtstandard.com

Helena Independent Record
www.helenair.com

Sidney Herald-Leader
www.sidneyherald.com

NEVADA

Las Vegas Review-Journal
www.lvrj.com

Nevada Appeal (Carson City)
www.nevadaappeal.com

Las Vegas Sun
www.lasvegassun.com

Reno Gazette-Journal
www.rgj.com

NEW MEXICO

Albuquerque Journal
www.abqjournal.com

Roswell Daily Record
www.roswell-record.com

The Albuquerque Tribune
www.abqtrib.com

The Santa Fe New Mexican
www.sfnewmexican.com

OKLAHOMA

The Edmond Evening Sun
www.edmondsun.com

The Oklahoman
www.newsok.com

The Lawton Constitution
www.lawton-constitution.com

Tulsa World
www.tulsaworld.com

OREGON

Corvallis Gazette-Times
www.gtconnect.com

The Daily Astorian
www.dailyastorian.com

Herald and News (Klamath Falls)
www.heraldandnews.com

Mail Tribune (Medford)
www.mailtribune.com

The News-Review (Roseburg)
www.oregonnews.com

The Oregonian (Portland)
www.oregonlive.com

The Register-Guard (Eugene)
www.registerguard.com

Statesman Journal (Salem)
http://news.statesmanjournal.com

TEXAS

Abilene Reporter-News
www.reporternews.com

Amarillo Globe-Times
www.amarillonet.com

Austin American-Statesman
www.austin360.com

Beaumont Enterprise
www.ent-net.com

Corpus Christi Caller-Times
www.caller.com

The Dallas Morning News
www.dallasnews.com

El Paso Times
www.elpasotimes.com

Gainesville Daily Register
www.gainesvilleregister.com

Galveston County Daily News
www.galvnews.com

Houston Chronicle
www.chron.com

Laredo Morning Times
www.lmtonline.com

Lubbock Avalanche-Journal
www.lubbockonline.com

Midland Reporter-Telegram
www.mywesttexas.com

San Angelo Standard-Times
www.texaswest.com

San Antonio Express-News
www.mysanantonio.com

Star-Telegram (Fort Worth)
www.star-telegram.com

Times News Record News (Wichita Falls)
www.trnonline.com

Waco Tribune-Herald
www.accesswaco.com

UTAH

The Daily Herald (Provo)
www.daily-herald.com

Deseret News (Salt Lake City)
www.deseretnews.com

The Salt Lake Tribune
www.sltrib.com

Standard-Examiner (Ogden)
www.standard.net

The Herald Journal
www.hjnews.com

The Utah County Journal
www.ucjournal.com

WASHINGTON

The Bellingham Herald
www.bellinghamherald.com
Eastside Journal (Bellevue)
www.eastsidejournal.com

Seattle Post-Intelligencer
www.seattle-pi.com
The Seattle Times
www.seattletimes.com

The Herald (Everett)
www.heraldnet.com

The Spokesman-Review (Spokane)
www.spokane.net

The News Tribune (Tacoma)
www.tribnet.com

Tri-City Herald
www.tri-cityherald.com

The Olympian (Olympia)
http://news.theolympian.com

Yakima Herald-Republic
www.yakima-herald.com

WYOMING

Casper Star-Tribune
www.trib.com

Wyoming Tribune-Eagle (Cheyenne)
www.wyomingnews.com

ALASKA JOBS CENTER

www.ilovealaska.com/alaskajobs
Number of job listings: Less than 250
Types of jobs: All
Locations of jobs: Alaska
Frequency of updates: As submitted
Search by: Help wanted category only
Resume database available: No
Employer profiles available: No
Costs for job seekers: Free
Costs for employers: Free
Other key features: Alaska's 100 largest employers list; state resources; national job listings link; and seasonal, volunteer, and training links.
Comments: Mixed with the few job ads were personal messages and some "opportunities" of questionable origin. The free ads, which are directly entered by the "employer," are not apparently screened for quality. Since Alaska's limited job market makes every resource precious, we are keeping this site listed, though we urge that you be cautious of the quality of these ads.

ALASKA, STATE OF

www.jobs.state.ak.us
Number of job listings: Over 5,000
Types of jobs: All
Locations of jobs: Alaska
Frequency of updates: Daily
Search by: Job category; Location
Resume database available: Yes
Employer profiles available: No
Costs for job seekers: Free
Costs for employers: Free
Other key features: Links to tips on interviewing, resumes, career fairs, and more.
Comments: There are several venues on this site to view job listings: Job seekers can view a list of the state jobs, federal jobs, fishing jobs, University of Alaska jobs, or the general job listings in the state generated from America's Job Bank.

BAJOBS.COM

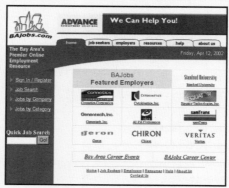

www.bajobs.com
Number of job listings: Over 1,000
Types of jobs: All
Locations of jobs: San Francisco Bay area
Frequency of updates: Daily
Search by: Date; Location; Keyword; Job category
Resume database available: Yes
Employer profiles available: Yes
Costs for job seekers: Free

Costs for employers: A single 30-day job posting is $100 for members, and $125 for nonmembers. Corporate memberships can be purchased on a weekly or quarterly basis and offer additional features such as preferred placement and resume bank access.

Other key features: Links to Bay Area employment and municipal resources.

Comments: This site is very well designed, clearly defining all its useful links no matter where you are in the site.

CLASSIFIEDS GATEWAY

www.sfna.com/classifieds
Number of job listings: Over 1,000
Types of jobs: All
Locations of jobs: San Francisco Bay area
Frequency of updates: Daily
Search by: Date posted; Keyword; Job category
Resume database available: No
Employer profiles available: No
Costs for job seekers: Free
Costs for employers: $295 per ad running 30 days with no restrictions on size.

Other key features: Job e-mail alerts and a "clip ads" system that allow users to create a list of the jobs for which they are interested in applying.

Comments: The online classifieds for several San Francisco area newspapers, including the *San Francisco Chronicle* and the *San Francisco Examiner*.

ColoradoJobs.com

www.coloradojobs.com
Number of job listings: Over 250
Types of jobs: All
Locations of jobs: Colorado
Frequency of updates: As submitted
Search by: Keyword; Job category
Resume database available: Yes
Employer profiles available: Yes
Costs for job seekers: Free
Costs for employers: $100 per ad running one month. Package deals are available. Contact site for details.
Other key features: You can browse through the entire jobs database with the listings sorted by city, job title, industry, or company. Links to salary and relocation information, and other job search sites.
Comments: Operated in partnership with KMGH-TV in Denver.

Jobnetwork.net

www.jobnetwork.net
Number of job listings: Over 800
Types of jobs: All
Locations of jobs: Los Angeles, San Francisco, San Diego, Las Vegas, and Orange County, CA
Frequency of updates: Daily
Search by: Location; Keyword
Resume database available: Yes
Employer profiles available: Yes
Costs for job seekers: Free
Costs for employers: $695 a year
Other key features: Virtual job fair; chat group; and online bulletin board.
Comments: This is actually a collection of five job search sites with the same layout and function, each focusing on a different metro area.

Montana Job Service

http://jsd.dli.state.mt.us
Types of jobs: All
Locations of jobs: Montana
Search by: Job category; Keyword; Date; Job title; Location

Resume database available: No
Employer profiles available: No
Costs for job seekers: Free
Costs for employers: Free
Other key features: A large resources page with links to information for both job seekers and employers, other job search engines, legislation, and associations.
Comments: This site is a service of the Montana Department of Labor and Industry.

OREGON EMPLOYMENT DEPARTMENT

www.emp.state.or.us
Number of job listings: Over 1,000
Types of jobs: All
Locations of jobs: Oregon
Frequency of updates: Daily
Search by: Job category; Keyword; Location; Date posted; Hours per week
Resume database available: No
Employer profiles available: No
Costs for job seekers: Free
Other key features: Includes links to state jobs, JOBS Plus (a program for needy families), and to America's Job Bank.
Comments: Provides a wealth of information for both job seekers and employers, and instructs both on how to use its services to find matches. Job seekers interested in a position must contact the office nearest them in order to apply for a position.

THE SILICON VALLEY JOB SOURCE

www.valleyjobs.com

Number of job listings: Over 1,000

Types of jobs: All, with a focus on computer and high-tech positions

Locations of jobs: California, primarily the Silicon Valley area

Frequency of updates:

Search by: Date posted; Job category; Keyword; Location

Resume database available: Yes

Employer profiles available: Yes

Costs for job seekers: Free

Costs for employers: $50 per ad running 60 days

Other key features: Links to venture capital firms and news sources in the Bay Area; apartment information; and free e-mail accounts.

680CAREERS.COM

www.680careers.com

Locations of jobs: California (Contra Costa and Alameda Counties)

Search by: Employer

Resume database available: No

Employer profiles available: Yes

Costs for job seekers: Free

Costs for employers: Free (certain restrictions apply)

Other key features: *Resubot* e-mail service allows job seekers to select a list of companies at the site, and e-mail a cover letter and resume to them; local information and resources; news of upcoming career fairs; and direct links to the employment pages of nearly 150 companies in the area.

Comments: Job seekers may look here to find links to major corporations in the 680 corridor of the above mentioned counties in California.

TODAY'S CAREERS

www.todays-careers.com
Number of job listings: Over 250
Types of jobs: All
Locations of jobs: Seattle
Frequency of updates: Daily online; Weekly in print
Search by: Job category; Keyword
Resume database available: Yes
Employer profiles available: Yes
Costs for job seekers: Free
Costs for employers: Start at $74 per column inch (with a minimum two-inch purchase). Ads appear in print version.
Other key features: Directory of employment services; listing of job fairs; calendar of events; general education and career information; an e-mail notification service; and archived articles.
Comments: Powered by CareerWeb.

TEXAS LOCAL OPENINGS

http://texas.localopenings.com
Number of job listings: Over 1,000
Types of jobs: All
Locations of jobs: Texas
Frequency of updates: Daily
Search by: Keyword; Job category; Date posted
Resume database available: Yes
Employer profiles available: No
Costs for job seekers: Free
Costs for employers: $125 per ad for 45 days; resumes sent free when employers register and indicate preferred candidate categories and locations.
Other key features: Links to other job sites.

WORKSOURCE WASHINGTON

www.wa.gov/esd/employment.html
Number of job listings: Over 4,500
Types of jobs: All
Locations of jobs: Washington state
Frequency of updates: Daily
Search by: Job category; Keyword; Location
Resume database available: Yes
Employer profiles available: No
Costs for job seekers: Free
Costs for employers: Free
Other key features: Information on wages; job information links; training programs; and an employers version of the site offering a variety of options.
Comments: This is a strong and easy-to-use site featuring a number of job postings and additional tools for job seekers in Washington state.

International Job Sites

AACI ISRAEL JOBNET

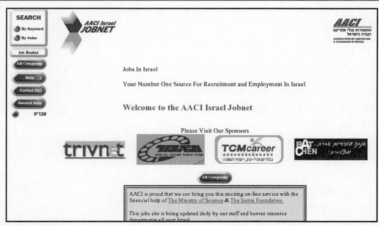

www.jobnet.co.il
Number of job listings: Over 1,000
Types of jobs: All
Locations of jobs: Israel
Frequency of updates: Daily
Search by: Company name; Job category; Location
Resume database available: No

Employer profiles available: Yes

Costs for job seekers: Free

Costs for employers: Contact site

Other key features: A dictionary of employment terms; database statistics; links to Israeli news; professional organizations; and jobs can be viewed in English or Hebrew.

ASIA-NET

www.asia-net.com

Number of job listings: Under 250

Types of jobs: All, with a focus on business and technical positions

Locations of jobs: Asia/Pacific Rim, including Australia and New Zealand

Search by: Company name; Job category; Keyword; Language; Location; Job title

Resume database available: Yes

Employer profiles available: No

Costs for job seekers: Free

Costs for employers: Contact site

Other key features: Links in ads to e-mail jobs to yourself or a friend.

Comments: Languages involved are Japanese, Chinese, Korean, and English.

ATLANTIC CANADA CAREERS

www.atlanticcanadacareers.com

Number of job listings: Over 250

Types of jobs: All

Locations of jobs: Eastern Canada

Frequency of updates: Daily

Search by: Job category; Location

Resume database available: No

Employer profiles available: Yes

Costs for job seekers: Free

Costs for employers: Contact site

Other key features: Links to schools and associations; a job notifier; and a free e-newsletter.

AUSTRALIAN JOB SEARCH

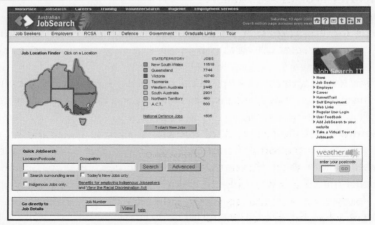

http://jobsearch.deetya.gov.au

Number of job listings: Over 10,000

Types of jobs: All

Locations of jobs: Australia

Frequency of updates: Daily

Search by: Industry; Job category; Location; Indigenous only; Keyword; Job type

Resume database available: Yes

Employer profiles available: No

Costs for job seekers: Free

Costs for employers: Contact site

Other key features: E-mail notification service; and a job resource section with links to other career-related sites.

Comments: This site is a service of the Australian Government and is only open to postings from Australian companies. The site's clean design and user-friendly links make it a must-see for anyone interested in employment in Australia.

BYRON EMPLOYMENT AUSTRALIA

http://employment.byron.com.au

Number of job listings:

Types of jobs: All

Locations of jobs: Australia

Frequency of updates:

Search by: Job category; Keyword; Location

Resume database available: No
Employer profiles available: No
Costs for job seekers: Free
Costs for employers: Starts at $30 per ad running four weeks; the price decreases per ad as you increase the number of postings per month.
Other key features: Links to other career resources; JobMail e-mail notification service; and insightful information for people interested in working in Australia.
Comments: A big drawback of this site is that the generated list of jobs are in the form of a list of links. The list only includes the job title and a short phrase that ineffectively describes the position. Still, this site is probably the most comprehensive job listing site focused on Australia, so with a little patience job seekers should find what they are looking for here.

CANADA JOB CENTRE

www.canadajobcentre.com
Number of job listings: Under 250
Types of jobs: All
Locations of jobs: Primarily Canada, with some international
Frequency of updates: Daily
Search by: Job category; Keyword; Location; Job title
Resume database available: Yes
Employer profiles available: Yes
Costs for job seekers: Free
Costs for employers: Free
Other key features: Anonymous resume posting.
Comments: This site was recently launched to replace the "jobs" section of canadacentre.com, and judging from the number of job and resume inquiries, it is becoming increasingly popular with both job seekers and employers.

THE CANADIAN JOBS CATALOGUE

www.kenevacorp.mb.ca
Number of job listings: Over 95,000
Types of jobs: All
Locations of jobs: Canada
Search by: Keyword; Job category

Resume database available: Yes
Costs for job seekers: $10 membership fee
Costs for employers: $10 membership fee
Comments: This site acts literally as a job catalogue, with a table of contents and links to sub-categories, locations, and cross-references. Rather than traditional job listings, the Canadian Jobs Catalogue identifies listings on employer Web sites.

CANADIAN RESUME CENTRE

www.canres.com
Number of job listings: Under 250
Types of jobs: All
Locations of jobs: Canada and some international
Frequency of updates: Daily
Search by: Job category; Location
Resume database available: Yes
Employer profiles available: No
Costs for job seekers: Free
Costs for employers: $25 for a three-month posting, or $50 for a confidential posting.
Other key features: Links to other career sites.

CAREER INDIA

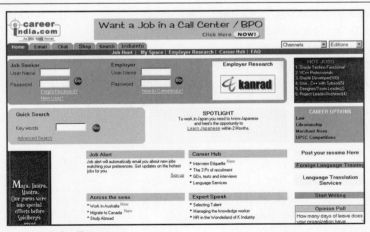

www.careerindia.com
Number of job listings: Under 250
Types of jobs: All

Locations of jobs: India and some international
Frequency of updates: As submitted
Search by: Job category; Location; Experience; Keyword
Resume database available: Yes
Employer profiles available: Yes
Costs for job seekers: Free
Costs for employers: Contact site
Other key features: Tips and news for job seekers and employers; message boards; and an e-mail job notification service.

CYBER INDIA ONLINE

www.cioljobs.com
Number of job listings: Over 500
Types of jobs: Computers
Locations of jobs: India, United States, and other international
Frequency of updates: Daily
Search by: Company; Keyword; Job category
Resume database available: Yes
Employer profiles available: Yes
Costs for job seekers: Free
Costs for employers: Membership registration is $225 for three months, $300 for six months, or $500 for a year. Other fees apply for posting jobs and viewing resumes.
Other key features: An assortment of "Message Boards" designed for employers, job seekers, and general IT professionals to share their views; relocation information; weekly polls; and a variety of other career resources.

FREE-JOB-SEARCH-ENGINES.COM

www.free-job-search-engines.com
Types of jobs: All
Locations of jobs: Australia, United Kingdom, United States, Hong Kong, and Canada
Search by: Keyword; Location; Search engine
Resume database available: No
Employer profiles available: No
Costs for job seekers: Free

Comments: This site utilizes several popular job search engines, seeking out opportunities in designated areas and compiling them for job seekers.

GAIJINPOT

www.gaijinpot.com
Number of job listings: Under 250
Types of jobs: All
Locations of jobs: Japan
Frequency of updates: Daily
Search by: Job category; Keyword
Resume database available: Yes
Employer profiles available: No
Costs for job seekers: Free
Costs for employers: 12,000 yen per job for 60 days
Other key features: Site user statistics for employers; resources on living in Japan; advice; forums; and informational columns.
Comments: GaijinPot offers a nice selection of additional resources useful to people interested in moving to and working in Japan.

GUARDIAN UNLIMITED

www.jobsunlimited.co.uk
Number of job listings: Over 3,000
Types of jobs: All
Locations of jobs: United Kingdom
Frequency of updates: Daily
Search by: Job category; Keyword; Location; Salary; Contract type; Date posted
Resume database available: Yes
Employer profiles available: No
Costs for job seekers: Free
Costs for employers: A wide variety of packages are available. Contact site for details.
Other key features: Links to other Guardian sites covering topics such as politics, sports, money, society, and more.

THE IRISH JOBS PAGE

www.irishjobs.ie

Number of job listings: Over 5,000

Types of jobs: All

Locations of jobs: Ireland

Frequency of updates: Daily

Search by: Job category; Keyword; Location; Recruiter type; Company name

Resume database available: Yes

Employer profiles available: Yes

Costs for job seekers: Free

Costs for employers: Contact site

Other key features: "My Jobs" allows job seekers to create their own personal section on the site in which they can receive updates about new job openings; the site can also be broken into a "Graduate" section and an "Executive" section, allowing for a more focused search.

Comments: As the leading career site in Ireland, IrishJobs offers both job seekers and employers a well-designed site with no shortage of resources.

JobServe

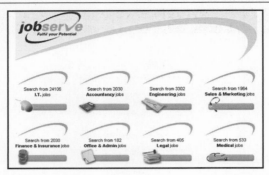

www.jobserve.com
Number of job listings: Over 35,000
Types of jobs: IT, Accounting, Marketing, Insurance, Office, Legal, and Medical
Locations of jobs: United Kingdom and some other international
Frequency of updates: Daily
Search by: Job category; Date posted; Job type; Keyword
Resume database available: Yes
Employer profiles available: No
Costs for job seekers: Free
Costs for employers: Contact site
Other key features: Links to recruiter and employer Web sites.
Comments: This site has become more streamlined since our last review, focusing primarily on job listings and cutting back on the extras.

Jobsite Group

www.jobsite.co.uk
Number of job listings: Over 25,000
Types of jobs: All
Locations of jobs: United Kingdom and international
Frequency of updates: Daily
Search by: Location; Job type; Job title; Job category; Date posted
Resume database available: Yes
Employer profiles available: Yes
Costs for job seekers: Free
Costs for employers: Contact site
Other key features: E-mail notification service and online job application.

JobStreet.com

www.jobstreet.com
Number of job listings: Over 20,000
Types of jobs: All
Locations of jobs: Singapore; India; Malaysia; Philippines; and some international
Frequency of updates: Daily
Search by: Industry; Keyword; Location
Resume database available: Yes
Employer profiles available: Yes
Costs for job seekers: Free
Costs for employers: Contact site
Other key features: Career advice and an e-mail notification service.
Comments: This site offers mirror sites in the United States, which helps speed up the connection for Internet users in North America. Free registration is required to make full use of the site's benefits.

Jobworld UK

www.jobworld.co.uk
Number of job listings: Over 20,000
Types of jobs: All
Locations of jobs: United Kingdom and international
Frequency of updates: Daily
Search by: Job category; Job type; Salary; Job title; Location
Resume database available: Yes
Employer profiles available: Yes
Costs for job seekers: Free

Costs for employers: Contact site

Other key features: Career news; *Skillswatch* advice guide; resume and interviewing tips; salary information; and more.

Comments: This is an extensive site offering a wealth of options and features to job seekers.

Monster.co.uk

www.monster.co.uk
Number of job listings: Over 20,000
Types of jobs: All
Locations of jobs: United Kingdom, Scotland, and Europe
Frequency of updates: Daily
Search by: Location; Job category; Job type; Keyword
Resume database available: Yes
Employer profiles available: Yes
Costs for job seekers: Free
Costs for employers: $250 for a 60-day posting
Other key features: Job search agent; communities; articles; advice; books; and more.
Comments: This is the United Kingdom version of the immensely popular Monster.com job search site.

NetJobs

www.netjobs.com
Number of job listings: Over 1,000
Types of jobs: All
Locations of jobs: Canada and the United States
Frequency of updates: Daily
Search by: Company; Job title; Job category; Location
Resume database available: Yes
Employer profiles available: No
Costs for job seekers: Free
Costs for employers: Ranges from $20 per job per month to $600 for unlimited postings and resume access for a year.
Comments: NetJobs is a basic no-frills job search site.

OVERSEAS JOBS EXPRESS

www.overseasjobs.com

Number of job listings: Over 250

Types of jobs: All

Locations of jobs: International

Frequency of updates: As submitted

Search by: Job category; Keyword; Location

Resume database available: Yes

Employer profiles available: Yes

Costs for job seekers: Free

Costs for employers: Free

Other key features: Tips and advice for living and working overseas; guide to career sites; and links to internship and resort opportunities.

Comments: This site is primarily targeted towards Americans interested in working in other countries. Overseas Jobs Express is part of the AboutJobs.com Network.

PEOPLEBANK

www.peoplebank.com

Number of job listings: Over 500

Types of jobs: All

Locations of jobs: United Kingdom and some international

Frequency of updates: Daily

Search by: Keyword; Salary; Location; Date; Job category

Resume database available: Yes

Employer profiles available: No

Costs for job seekers: Free

Costs for employers: Contact site

Other key features: The job seeker advice center features interview advice, articles, opinions, and legal information.

STEPSTONE

StepStone
your career. your life. your future.

Europe's online career and HR service

Austria Belgium Denmark Finland France Germany Italy Luxembourg
Netherlands Norway Portugal Sweden Switzerland United Kingdom

International   Investor Relations

www.stepstone.ie

Number of job listings: Varies

Types of jobs: All

Locations of jobs: Europe

Frequency of updates: Daily

Search by: Company name; Job category; Job type; Keyword; Location

Costs for job seekers: Free

Costs for employers: Contact site

Other key features: Education links; career advice.

Comments: This Web address is the portal to a number of linked Stepstone job sites for 14 European countries, including Austria, Belgium, France, Switzerland, and the United Kingdom. Most sites are in the language of the country, and available services will very by site.

TOP JOBS ON THE NET

www.topjobs.co.uk

Number of job listings: Over 1,000

Types of jobs: All

Locations of jobs: United Kingdom

Frequency of updates: Daily

Search by: Job category; Location; Date posted; Keyword

Resume database available: No

Employer profiles available: Yes

Costs for job seekers: Free

Costs for employers: Contact site

Other key features: Career tips; an online job magazine; career management advice; psychometric tests; book reviews; and tips on how to dress.

Comments: The career advice section of this site is truly impressive, with a lot of useful information for job seekers.

VACANCIES

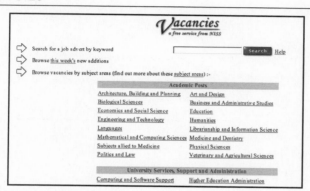

www.vacancies.ac.uk

Number of job listings: Less than 250

Types of jobs: Higher education

Locations of jobs: Primarily the United Kingdom

Frequency of updates: As submitted

Search by: Job category

Resume database available: No

Employer profiles available: No

Costs for job seekers: Free

Costs for employers: Free

Comments: Temporary and research positions are also included on this site.

WORKOPOLIS.COM

www.workopolis.com

Number of job listings: Over 20,000

Types of jobs: All

Locations of jobs: Canada

Frequency of updates: Daily

Search by: Job category; Keyword; Date posted; Industry

Resume database available: Yes

Employer profiles available: Some

Costs for job seekers: Free

Costs for employers: Contact site

Other key features: CareerAlert e-mail notification service; articles; advice; an MBA program search; and Worknet Unique, an online training service.

Comments: Workopolis is available in both English and French.

CHAPTER FIVE

JOB SITES FOR SPECIFIC CAREERS

Most people already know which field they would like to find a job in, so it makes sense to make the most of those resources geared just to your particular industry. The sites presented in this chapter provide a wealth of industry-specific job listings; some also provide links to industry publications, discussion boards, and other resources. For those just starting out who are still considering several different fields, or for anyone considering a career change, these sites are a good place to start when investigating what kinds of jobs are available in particular industries.

Some of the sites listed here are from national organizations such as the National Association of Broadcasters (**www.nab.org/bcc**). The names and Web sites of a number of additional professional organizations are listed at the end of Chapter Eight. Besides the job listings they might provide, industry organization sites can be helpful in other ways. You can use them to keep updated about news in your industry, find out more about the prominent companies and people in a field, and learn about professional memberships that might further your career development.

A few of the sites in this chapter are geographically specific, such as TeachGeorgia.org (**www.teachgeorgia.org**) for positions in Georgia schools, or International Pharmajobs (**www.pharmajobs.com**), which has only European biotechnology and pharmaceutical jobs. If you want to limit your job search geographically yourself, many national sites have features that allow you to search by location.

Industry-Specific Sites
Accounting/Banking/Finance

ACCOUNTING.COM

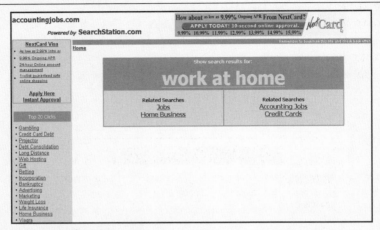

www.accounting.com

Number of job listings: Over 250

Types of jobs: Accounting

Locations of jobs: United States

Frequency of updates: As submitted

Search by: Company name; Job category; Keyword; Location

Resume database available: Yes

Employer profiles available: Yes

Costs for job seekers: Free

Costs for employers: $45 per ad running one month. Resumes can be searched for $175 for two months with the "Bronze" package, which also allows for up to five job listings for $35 each. At the time of this writing, Accounting.com was offering free listings in their CPA directory.

Other key features: Discussion groups; links to associations and state CPA boards; and helpful tips on writing a resume.

ASSOCIATION FOR
FINANCIAL PROFESSIONALS

www.afponline.org

Number of job listings: Over 250

Types of jobs: Financial services

Locations of jobs: United States
Search by: Keyword; Job type; Job level; Location; Date posted
Resume database available: No
Employer profiles available: Yes
Costs for job seekers: Free to members; membership is $295 per year.
Costs for employers: Either $500 for unlimited job postings for a month, or $5,000 for unlimited job postings for a year.
Other key features: The main site offers sections on professional development, an information center, and financial tools.

BANKJOBS.COM

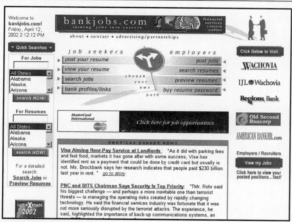

www.bankjobs.com
Number of job listings: Over 5,000
Types of jobs: Banking; Financial services
Locations of jobs: United States
Frequency of updates: Daily
Search by: Keyword; Location
Resume database available: Yes
Employer profiles available: Yes
Costs for job seekers: Free
Costs for employers: $45 per posting, or five postings for $200.
Other key features: American banking news; anonymous resumes; and links to lots of other banking-related sites.

BLOOMBERG.COM

www.bloomberg.com/careers

Number of job listings: Less than 250

Types of jobs: Financial services

Locations of jobs: United States and some international

Frequency of updates: Daily

Search by: Job category; Keyword; Location; Salary; Date posted

Resume database available: Yes

Employer profiles available: No

Costs for job seekers: Free

Costs for employers: Contact site

Other key features: E-mail notification service; links to the various sections of the main Bloomberg.com site, offering information on money, life, broadcasting, and more.

CFO.COM

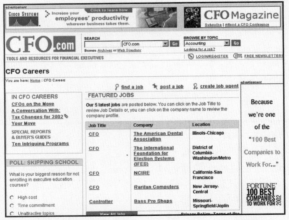

www.cfo.com/career

Number of job listings: Under 250

Types of jobs: Financial services, primarily the positions of chief financial officer, treasurer, and senior financial executive

Locations of jobs: United States

Frequency of updates: Daily

Search by: Location; Job category; Job type; Keyword

Resume database available: No

Employer profiles available: No

Costs for job seekers: Free

Costs for employers: Contact site
Other key features: Job search agent; free e-newsletter; and additional tools and resources for financial executives on the main CFO.com site.
Comments: While this site does not offer a multitude of jobs, individuals interested in high-ranking positions in a financial institution would be well served to look here.

FINANCIALJOBS.COM

www.financialjobs.com
Number of job listings: Under 250
Types of jobs: Accounting; Financial services
Locations of jobs: United States
Frequency of updates: Daily
Search by: Keyword; Location; Salary; Experience; Job type; Experience
Resume database available: Yes
Employer profiles available: No
Costs for job seekers: Free
Costs for employers: $353 per listing for 90 days
Other key features: Numerous articles
Comments: Registration is required to apply for jobs.

FINCAREER.COM

www.fincareer.com
Types of jobs: Financial services
Locations of jobs: United States and some international
Frequency of updates: Daily
Search by: Job type; Location; Keyword; Experience
Resume database available: Yes
Employer profiles available:
Costs for job seekers: Free
Costs for employers: Free
Comments: Rather than full resumes, this site offers profiles of job seekers that employers can search through.

JOBSINTHEMONEY

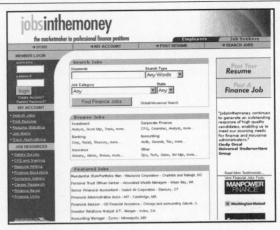

www.jobsinthemoney.com

Number of job listings: Over 250

Types of jobs: Financial services

Locations of jobs: United States and some international

Frequency of updates: Daily

Search by: Job category; Keyword; Location

Resume database available: Yes

Employer profiles available: Yes

Costs for job seekers: Free

Costs for employers: Contact site

Other key features: Jobs are listed by date posted; a privacy policy that includes anonymous resumes and Company Hide, which allows job seekers to show their resume only to approved companies.

Comments: Many of the jobs posted were from employment agencies. The company profiles are informative, with such details as contact information, a link to the company's Web site, and a brief description.

NATIONAL BANKING NETWORK

www.banking-financejobs.com

Types of jobs: Banking; Financial services

Locations of jobs: United States and some international

Frequency of updates: Weekly

Search by: Job category; Location

Resume database available: Yes
Employer profiles available: No
Costs for job seekers: Free, but registration is required for access.
Costs for employers: Contact site
Comments: This Web site represents an association of independently owned recruiting firms specializing in the banking and financial service industries. If you prefer to deal directly with companies, this may not be the site for you.

Advertising/Marketing/Public Relations

AdWeekOnline Career Network

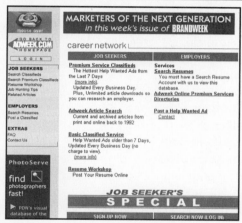

www.adweek.com
Number of job listings: Over 250
Types of jobs: Advertising; Marketing; Public relations; Publishing
Locations of jobs: United States
Frequency of updates: Weekly
Search by: Company name; Job category; Keyword; Location
Resume database available: Yes
Employer profiles available: No
Costs for job seekers: Free for basic access; $14.95 a month for premium access
Costs for employers: Contact site
Other key features: Online access to the Adweek Directory, Brandweek Directory, Mediaweek Directory, and IQ (interactive/new media) Directory.
Comments: This is the online version of AdWeek magazine.

MARKETINGJOBS.COM

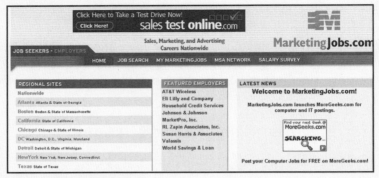

www.marketingjobs.com
Number of job listings: Under 250
Types of jobs: Advertising; Marketing; Sales
Locations of jobs: United States
Frequency of updates: Daily
Search by: Job type; Keyword; Location
Resume database available: Yes
Employer profiles available: Yes
Costs for job seekers: Free
Costs for employers: $150 per ad running one month. Packages start at $495 per month and include unlimited job postings, a company profile, and resume access.
Other key features: The MSA Network features links to ad agencies, associations, career information, and more.
Comments: This site does a good job of telling you what it offers, how much of it is available, and all the costs involved. The number of listings for each job category is impressive and clearly defined.

MARKETINGPOWER.COM

www.marketingpower.com
Number of job listings: Over 500
Types of jobs: Marketing
Locations of jobs: United States
Frequency of updates: As submitted
Search by: Date posted; Keyword; Location; Job level; Job type; Salary
Resume database available: Yes
Employer profiles available: No
Costs for job seekers: Free

Costs for employers: $150 for a single post for 30 days. Discounts for multiple postings are also available.

Other key features: Job search agent; confidential profile; resume distribution; and relocation information.

Comments: This is the official Web site of the American Marketing Association.

MARKETING RESEARCH ASSOCIATION

www.mra-net.org
Number of job listings: Less than 250
Types of jobs: Marketing
Locations of jobs: United States
Frequency of updates: Monthly
Search by: Keyword
Resume database available: No
Employer profiles available: No
Costs for job seekers: Free
Costs for employers: Contact site
Other key features: Links to distance learning and video training programs.
Comments: Job ads also appear in the printed newsletter *Alert!*

THE NATIONAL DIVERSITY
NEWSPAPER JOB BANK

www.newsjobs.com
Number of job listings: Under 250
Types of jobs: Newspaper positions including advertising, marketing, journalism, editorial, and public relations, specifically for minority groups.
Locations of jobs: United States
Frequency of updates: Daily
Search by: Location; Experience; Medium; Circulation size
Resume database available: Yes
Employer profiles available: No
Costs for job seekers: Free
Costs for employers: Free
Other key features: All resumes are reviewed for content.
Comments: Job seekers must register and submit a resume in order to view job openings.

PUBLIC RELATIONS
SOCIETY OF AMERICA

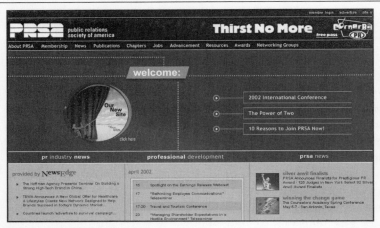

www.prsa.org/career

Number of job listings: Under 250

Types of jobs: Public relations

Locations of jobs: United States

Frequency of updates: Weekly

Search by: Location

Resume database available: Yes

Employer profiles available: No

Costs for job seekers: Free to search jobs; free to post a resume if you are a PRSA member. If not, the cost is $40 to post a resume for a three-month period. Membership requires a $65 initiation fee and $225 in annual dues.

Costs for employers: Classified ads are $155 for the first five lines. Each additional line is $20. The ads run for one month.

Other key features: Calendar of events; career information for the PR professional; a directory of PR firms; and a listing of PR links.

Comments: This site is a solid resource for anyone interested in the public relations industry.

Aerospace

THE AIRLINE EMPLOYMENT ASSISTANCE
CORPS & AVJOBS WORLDWIDE

www.avjobs.com

Number of job listings: Over 1,000

Types of jobs: Airline; Airport; Aviation; and Aerospace

Locations of jobs: United States

Frequency of updates: Daily

Search by: Category; Location; Job title; Company; Keyword

Resume database available: Yes

Employer profiles available: No

Costs for job seekers: $19.95 for basic membership; $24.95 for membership with resume privileges.

Costs for employers: Free

Other key features: The Crew Room aviation chat center; aviation career overviews; information on requirements; and statistics on aviation jobs.

AVIATIONEMPLOYMENT.COM

www.aviationemployment.com

Number of job listings: Over 500

Types of jobs: Aviation

Locations of jobs: United States

Search by: Location; Education; Job category; Job type; Salary

Resume database available: Yes

Employer profiles available: Yes

Costs for job seekers: Free

Costs for employers: $95 per ad for 30 days; package deals are also available.

Other key features: School profiles; links to *Pilot Employment News* and *Aviation Maintenance & Engineering Journal*.

Space Jobs

www.spacejobs.com

Number of job listings: Less than 250

Types of jobs: Aerospace

Locations of jobs: United States and some international

Frequency of updates: Daily

Search by: Company; Keyword; Location; Job category; Job title; Salary; Degree of travel desired; Education level; Relocation cost coverage

Resume database available: Yes

Employer profiles available: Yes

Costs for job seekers: Free

Costs for employers: Contact site

Other key features: E-mail notification service; a schedule of related conferences; and a list of events relating to the aerospace industry.

Agriculture

AMERICAN SOCIETY OF AGRICULTURAL ENGINEERS

www.asae.org

Number of job listings: Less than 250

Types of jobs: Agriculture

Locations of jobs: United States

Frequency of updates: Monthly

Resume database available: No

Employer profiles available: No

Costs for job seekers: Free; members receive a two-month "Positions Wanted" listing free; nonmembers must pay $55 per month to post an ad.

Costs for employers: Contact site

Other key features: All employment ads also appear in the print version of *Resource* magazine.

Comments: Membership rates range from $19 to $110, depending on age and education.

Arts and Entertainment

ART JOB

www.artjob.org

Number of job listings: Less than 250

Types of jobs: The arts, including full-time, part-time, internships, grant opportunities, and calls for entry

Locations of jobs: United States and some international

Frequency of updates: Daily

Resume database available: Yes

Employer profiles available: Yes

Costs for job seekers: $25 for three months

Costs for employers: A 30-day job posting is $45 for nonprofit organizations and $75 for commercial employers.

Other key features: Articles and links to related sites

Comments: While the cost is prohibitive for some people, this site does seem to offer unique job opportunities for a select job market.

CASTING DAILY

www.castingdaily.com

Number of job listings: Over 300

Types of jobs: Acting roles including film, television, stage, commercials, and voice-overs

Locations of jobs: United States, primarily New York and Los Angeles

Frequency of updates: Daily

Resume database available: Yes

Employer profiles available: No

Costs for job seekers: $19.95 per month for membership that includes access to casting notices, a spot for a resume, and access to Background Players.

Costs for employers: Free

Other key features: Covers both principal roles and background players too.

Comments: You can open a one-week trial membership for $9.95. Actors/Actresses can open a Virtual Portfolio, which includes headshots, introductory page, and resume.

CREW NET

www.crewnet.com

Number of job listings: Over 300

Types of jobs: Crew production jobs in the entertainment industry

Locations of jobs: Majority are located in Los Angeles and New York

Frequency of updates: Daily

Resume database available: Yes

Employer profiles available: No

Costs for job seekers: $19.95 per month for membership that includes access to job openings, resume posting, and an e-mail account.

Costs for employers: Free to list projects. Paid advertising is also available. Contact site for details.

Comments: You can open a one-week trial membership for $9.95.

The Internet Music Pages

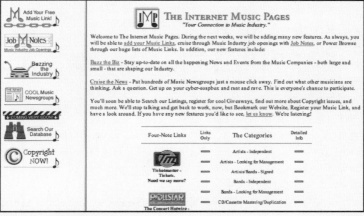

www.musicpages.com

Types of jobs: Music, mainly technical positions

Locations of jobs: United States and some international

Search by: Company name

Resume database available: No

Employer profiles available: No

Costs for job seekers: Free

Costs for employers: Contact site

Other key features: A well-organized system of every music-related link imaginable, from music education to indie labels; and links to music-related newsgroups.

Comments: This site posts links to the employment sections of corporate Web sites.

Online Sports

www.onlinesports.com/careercenter.html

Types of jobs: Sports and Recreation

Locations of jobs: United States

Frequency of updates: Biweekly

Resume database available: Yes

Employer profiles available: No

Costs for job seekers: Free

Costs for employers: Free; resumes can be viewed for free in a list format.

Other key features: Links to other job search information sites.

Comments: The resume section of this site only allows for an unsearchable list of job seekers.

SHOWBIZJOBS.COM

www.showbizjobs.com

Number of job listings: Over 100

Types of jobs: Show business, including entertainment, production, and administrative positions

Locations of jobs: United States

Frequency of updates: Daily

Search by: Location; Job category; Keyword; Salary; Company name; Date

Resume database available: Yes

Employer profiles available: Yes

Costs for job seekers: Free to search jobs; $35 for premium membership, which gives you access to additional features and lets you post a resume for six months.

Costs for employers: $125 per ad running one month. Bulk posting and membership rates that include resume searches are also available.

Other key features: "Send job to a friend," "Showbizjobs Runner" e-mail notification service, and chat and message boards.

Comments: The job listings are primarily for behind-the-scenes positions.

TALENTWORKS

www.talentworks.com

Types of jobs: Acting, performing arts

Locations of jobs: United States
Frequency of updates: Daily
Resume database available: Yes
Costs for job seekers: $49.99 per year for an individual subscription.
Costs for employers: Membership is not required to post casting calls. Advertising packages are available. Contact site for details.
Other key features: Membership includes a spot on the site to post a resume with a headshot (actors/actresses will have a specific URL for their page). The site also includes a chat room.

Biotechnology/Scientific

ACADEMIC PHYSICIAN & SCIENTIST

www.acphysci.com
Number of job listings: Over 400
Types of jobs: Academic positions in medicine and science
Locations of jobs: United States
Frequency of updates: Bimonthly
Search by: Keyword; Job category; Location
Resume database available: No
Employer profiles available: No
Costs for job seekers: Free
Costs for employers: Contact site
Comments: In addition to the Web site, there is a bimonthly publication that lists recruitment news and classified advertising in academic medicine. Subscription to the publication is free to all members of the academic medical community residing in the United States.

AMERICAN ASTRONOMICAL SOCIETY

www.aas.org
Number of job listings: Fewer than 250
Types of jobs: Astronomy
Locations of jobs: United States and some international
Frequency of updates: Monthly
Search by: Keyword
Resume database available: Yes
Employer profiles available: No
Costs for job seekers: Free
Costs for employers: $109 per ad running one month
Other key features: Links to a few other similar career sites; listings of summer jobs, fellowships, and other student opportunities; and extensive links to various related journals and publications.

AMERICAN INSTITUTE OF PHYSICS

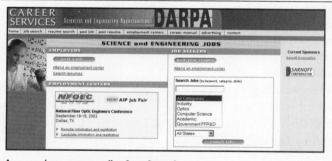

www.aip.org/careersvc/index.html
Number of job listings: Over 200
Types of jobs: Physicist positions in academia, industry, and government
Locations of jobs: United States
Frequency of updates: Daily
Search by: Keyword; Category; Location
Resume database available: Yes
Employer profiles available: No
Costs for job seekers: Free
Costs for employers: $18 per line, with a five-line minimum. Ads run for one month.
Other key features: Extensive information on industry events, salary and industry statistics; and links to online science journals.

THE BIOCAREER CENTER

www.biocareer.com

Number of job listings: Over 200

Types of jobs: Biotechnology

Locations of jobs: United States

Search by: Company name; Location; Job type; Job title; Keyword

Resume database available: Yes

Employer profiles available: Yes

Costs for job seekers: Free

Costs for employers: $150 per ad for the first two months, then $75 per ad each month thereafter. Bulk discounts are also available. Academic postdoctoral listings are free.

Other key features: Discussion boards; career advice; articles; and links to other online resources.

Comments: This site is part of the SciWeb network of sites.

BIO ONLINE

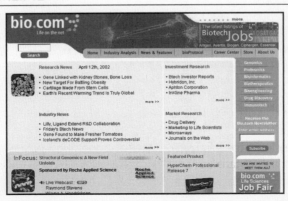

http://www.bio.com
Number of job listings: Over 1,000
Types of jobs: Life sciences
Locations of jobs: United States and some international
Frequency of updates: Daily
Search by: Keyword; Company name; Job type; Location; Skills; Experience; Date posted; Education; Salary
Resume database available: Yes
Employer profiles available: Yes
Costs for job seekers: Free
Costs for employers: $185 per ad running one month. The cost for renewal is $135 per job per month.
Other key features: Links to industry news and activities; job fair schedules; links to research and education sources; and an open forum discussion area.

THE BIOSPACE CAREER CENTER

www.biospace.com/career_main.cfm
Types of jobs: Biotechnology
Locations of jobs: United States and some international
Search by: Job category; Location; Keyword; Company name
Resume database available: No
Employer profiles available: Mini-profiles that include the company's address, a current stock quote, key statistics, and Web site links are available.
Costs for job seekers: Free
Costs for employers: $175 per ad per month for non-exhibitors, and $125 per ad per month for exhibitors.
Other key features: Information on industry news, events, and resources.
Comments: Check out the Career Center links on the left sidebar of the site's home page for advanced search options. One problem with this site is you cannot connect between job openings and company profiles or vice versa.

INTERNATIONAL PHARMAJOBS

www.pharmajobs.com
Types of jobs: Biotechnology; Pharmaceutical
Locations of jobs: Europe
Frequency of updates:
Search by: Job category; Location; Company name
Resume database available: Yes
Employer profiles available: No
Costs for job seekers: Free
Costs for employers: 250 euro per ad for eight weeks.
Other key features: E-mail notification service costing $32 for six
months.
Comments: This site does not feature any employment opportunities
in the United States.

PHYSICSJOBS

http://physicsweb.org/jobs
Number of job listings: Less than 250
Types of jobs: Physics
Locations of jobs: United States and some international
Frequency of updates: Daily
Search by: Keyword; Location; Job category; Salary
Resume database available: Yes
Employer profiles available: No
Costs for job seekers: Free
Costs for employers: Contact site
Other key features: E-mail notification service and a links to a variety
of news and resources related to the field of physics.

SCIENCE CAREERS

www.sciencecareers.org
Number of job listings: Over 600
Types of jobs: Scientific
Locations of jobs: United States and some international
Frequency of updates: Weekly
Search by: Keyword; Discipline; Location; Job category; Organization
Resume database available: Yes
Employer profiles available: Yes
Costs for job seekers: Free
Costs for employers: Contact site
Other key features: Information on career fairs; career advice; and a section dedicated to academic connections.
Comments: Affiliated with *Science* magazine.

SCIENCE JOBS

www.sciencejobs.com
Number of job listings: Over 400
Types of jobs: Bioscience and chemistry
Locations of jobs: United States and some international
Frequency of updates: Daily
Search by: Field; Sector; Discipline; Location; Date posted; Keyword
Resume database available: Yes
Employer profiles available: No
Costs for job seekers: Free
Costs for employers: $175 for academic positions, $275 for all other positions
Other key features: E-mail job search agent; links to related information on other sites.
Comments: Owned by the publishers of BioMedNet, Cell, NewScientist, and ChemWeb.com.

Charities and Social Services

ACCESS

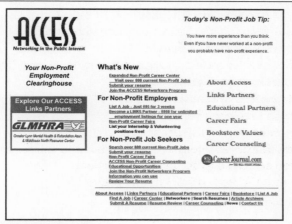

www.communityjobs.org

Number of job listings: Less than 250

Types of jobs: Nonprofits; Charities

Locations of jobs: United States and some international

Frequency of updates: Three times a week

Search by: Keyword; Company name; Job title; Job description; Position type; Location

Resume database available: No

Employer profiles available: Links to organization Web sites within ads

Costs for job seekers: Free

Costs for employers: Start at $95 per ad running three weeks. No charge for internships and volunteer positions.

Other key features: Information on nonprofit career fairs; articles; and an online bookstore.

CHARITY CHANNEL

www.charitychannel.com/careersearch/
Number of job listings: Less than 250
Types of jobs: Nonprofits; Charities
Locations of jobs: United States and some international
Frequency of updates: As submitted
Search by: Job title; Location; Organization name; Classification
Resume database available: No
Employer profiles available: No
Costs for job seekers: Free
Costs for employers: $155 per search
Other key features: Job listings are included in their weekly e-mail newsletter.

COMMUNITY CAREER CENTER

www.nonprofitjobs.org
Number of job listings: Over 250
Types of jobs: Nonprofits
Locations of jobs: United States and some international
Frequency of updates: Daily
Search by: Date; Location; Affiliation; Job skills; Job category; Job title; Keyword; Date posted
Resume database available: Candidate profiles are available
Employer profiles available: Yes
Costs for job seekers: Free
Costs for employers: $125 for one ad; $100 per ad for two or more; or $75 for five or more ads.
Other key features: Links to fundraising information; publications; international opportunities; faith-based initiatives; conferences; and more.

THE FEMINIST CAREER CENTER

www.feminist.org/911/jobs/911jobs.asp
Number of job listings: Less than 250
Types of jobs: Positions with nonprofit and social services organizations for feminist and progressive groups.
Locations of jobs: United States and some international
Frequency of updates: Every few days
Search by: Job title; Keyword; Organization; Date posted; Job type

Resume database available: Yes
Employer profiles available: No
Costs for job seekers: Free
Costs for employers: Free
Other key features: Links to a large number of various female resources, ranging from breast cancer to women in Afghanistan to women in sports.
Comments: This site is part of the Feminist Majority Foundation.

IDEALIST

www.idealist.org
Number of job listings: Over 1,000
Types of jobs: Community organizations; Nonprofits
Locations of jobs: United States and some international
Frequency of updates: Daily
Search by: Location; Job category; Keyword; Job type; Language; Date posted; Area of focus
Resume database available: No
Employer profiles available: Yes
Costs for job seekers: Free
Costs for employers: The costs for U.S. organizations is $40 per ad running indefinitely. International organizations can post free of charge.
Other key features: Job search agent; career fair information; free newsletter; and tools for organizations.
Comments: A project of Action Without Borders, Idealist is an online directory of nonprofit and volunteer resources.

MINISTRY CONNECT

www.ministryconnect.org
Number of job listings: Less than 250
Types of jobs: All, generally social service and other positions with nonprofits
Locations of jobs: United States and some international
Frequency of updates: Daily
Search by: Date; Job category; Location
Resume database available: Yes
Employer profiles available: No

Costs for job seekers: Free to search jobs; $25 per month for resume posting.

Costs for employers: $25 per ad running one month. Bulk ad and membership rates are available. Some organizations may be eligible for *pro bono* services.

Other key features: Links to related sites.

NATIONAL ASSOCIATION
OF SOCIAL WORKERS

www.artofsearch.com/nasw
Number of job listings: Less than 250
Types of jobs: Social services
Locations of jobs: United States and some international
Frequency of updates: Daily
Search by: Job category; Keyword; Location
Resume database available: Yes
Employer profiles available: Yes
Costs for job seekers: Free
Costs for employers: Start at $195 per ad running one month. Bulk posting rates and packages that included resume access are also available.
Other key features: Links on the main NASW page include articles, continuing education, diversity and equity, social work myths, and a host of others.

NEW ENGLAND OPPORTUNITY NOCs

www.opnocsne.org
Number of job listings: Less than 250
Types of jobs: Nonprofits
Locations of jobs: New England
Frequency of updates: Daily
Search by: Job category
Resume database available: No
Employer profiles available: No
Costs for job seekers: Free
Costs for employers: Start at $125 for up to 300 words for 30 days.
Other key features: Internships and volunteer listings; an extensive list of links to nonprofit sites and various career resources Web sites.

NONPROFIT CAREER NETWORK

www.nonprofitcareer.com
Number of job listings: Less than 250
Types of jobs: Nonprofits
Locations of jobs: United States and some international
Frequency of updates:
Search by: Location; Job type
Resume database available: Yes
Employer profiles available: Yes
Costs for job seekers: Free; $40 per year to post a resume.
Costs for employers: Nonprofits can get a one year membership for an introductory rate of $495 (includes resume access and unlimited job postings). Individual job postings for for-profit organizations cost $125 for 60 days.
Other key features: A directory of nonprofit companies; a directory of professional services; a volunteer section; and a directory of job fairs, conferences, workshops, and conventions.

THE NONPROFIT TIMES ONLINE

www.nptimes.com
Number of job listings: Less than 250
Types of jobs: Charities; Social services; Nonprofits
Locations of jobs: United States
Frequency of updates: Monthly
Resume database available: No
Employer profiles available: No

Costs for job seekers: Free

Costs for employers: $1.70 per word for line ads, and $100 per column inch for display ads.

Other key features: A directory that includes the names and contact information of a wide range of nonprofit organizations.

OpportunityNOCS

www.opportunitynocs.org
Number of job listings: Over 700
Types of jobs: Nonprofits
Locations of jobs: United States
Frequency of updates: Daily
Search by: Keyword; Organization type; Location; Job title; Date posted
Resume database available: No
Employer profiles available: No
Costs for job seekers: Free
Costs for employers: $80 per ad running 30 days. There is no charge for the online listing if an ad is placed in the print version.
Other key features: Nonprofit library and career resource center; and links to newsgroups, employment sites, and nonprofit sites.
Comments: Brought to you by the same people who bring you *Opportunity NOCs*, the printed newsletter. The newsletter, with editions for Boston, New York, Philadelphia, and other metropolitan areas, details more than 1,000 new job listings each month to over 50,000 subscribers.

Peace Corps

www.peacecorps.gov/employment/index.cfm
Types of jobs: Volunteer
Locations of jobs: Worldwide
Frequency of updates: As submitted.
Search by: Opportunity type
Costs for job seekers: Free
Other key features: Positions can be applied for online; information on what types of positions are offered, required qualifications, and locations of various positions; and a list of recruiting events.
Comments: Most positions require a bachelor's degree or higher, a two-year commitment, and the candidate must be in good physical

shape. Positions offer full room and board, scholarship opportunities, and a stipend at the end of the job. Qualified people can also earn graduate school credit while on assignment.

SOCIALSERVICE.COM

www.socialservice.com

Types of jobs: Social services

Locations of jobs: United States

Frequency of updates: Daily

Search by: Location

Resume database available: No

Employer profiles available: No

Costs for job seekers: Free

Costs for employers: Vary, based on the number of positions advertised and how long the ad will run. A single job posting running for two weeks is $65.

Other key features: An e-mail notification service; and an assortment of job links to employers and employment agencies. Jobs are listed by state.

Comments: A good source for narrowing your search for social services jobs to a particular geographic area.

Communications

THE ASSOCIATION FOR MULTIMEDIA COMMUNICATIONS

www.amcomm.org
Number of job listings: Less than 250
Types of jobs: Multimedia communications, primarily Web designers
Locations of jobs: United States, primarily Chicago, IL
Frequency of updates: Daily
Search by: Date posted
Resume database available: No
Employer profiles available: No
Costs for job seekers: Free
Costs for employers: Free
Other key features: A directory of members

MEDIAPOST

www.mediapost.com
Number of job listings:
Types of jobs: Media and advertising
Locations of jobs: United States
Frequency of updates: Daily
Search by: Job category
Resume database available: No
Employer profiles available: No
Costs for job seekers: Free. Membership is required.
Costs for employers: Free up to 200 characters, then $.50 for each additional character. Membership is required.
Other key features: An all-media directory; news; tools; resources; and a vast number of links to related content.
Comments: Membership is free.

NATIONAL ASSOCIATION OF BROADCASTERS

www.nab.org/bcc
Number of job listings: Less than 250
Types of jobs: Broadcasting
Locations of jobs: United States

Frequency of updates: Daily
Search by: Position; Job category; Industry; Location; Date posted
Resume database available: Yes
Employer profiles available: No
Costs for job seekers: Free
Costs for employers: Free for members. Membership costs vary.
Other key features: Links to other broadcasting career sites; and notices of major upcoming events.
Comments: This site includes a useful resource center for people trying to break into the broadcasting field.

NEW MEDIA ASSOCIATION
OF NEW JERSEY

www.nmanj.com/classified/class.html
Number of job listings: Less than 250
Types of jobs: New Media, primarily Web designers
Locations of jobs: New Jersey and New York City
Frequency of updates: Daily
Resume database available: No
Employer profiles available: No
Costs for job seekers: Free
Costs for employers: Free
Other key features: A calendar of events, discussion forums, and a spotlight link, which contains various articles submitted by members. Members also have access to a fully directory of all members.
Comments: The site was offering free membership at the time of this writing.

SOCIETY FOR TECHNICAL
COMMUNICATION

www.stc.org/jobdatabase.htm

Number of job listings: Less than 250

Types of jobs: Technical communication, primarily tech writers and editors

Locations of jobs: United States and some international

Frequency of updates: Daily

Search by: Location; Salary; Job type

Resume database available: No

Employer profiles available: No

Costs for job seekers: Free

Costs for employers: Free

Other key features: Information on academics, conferences, books, periodicals, and salary; and links to related special interest groups.

TVJOBS.COM

www.tvjobs.com

Types of jobs: Television and Radio

Locations of jobs: United States

Frequency of updates: Daily

Search by: Job type; Job category; Date posted; Broadcast market; Station name; Station affiliation; Time zone; Region

Resume database available: Yes

Employer profiles available: Yes

Costs for job seekers: Membership starts at $10 per month.

Costs for employers: Free

Other key features: Internship database; master station index; directory of broadcast stations; freelance directory; tips on resume tapes; directory of station joblines; and career advice.

Computers

1-JOBS.COM

www.1-jobs.com

Number of job listings: Approximately 400

Types of jobs: Computers; Engineering; Telecommunications

Locations of jobs: United States and some international

Frequency of updates: Hourly

Search by: Keyword; Location; Date posted

Resume database available: Yes

Employer profiles available: Yes

Costs for job seekers: Free

Costs for employers: Contact site

Other key features: A schedule of high-tech career fairs

Comments: 1-Jobs.com is part of the Brass Ring Network, which at the time of this writing, seemed to be undergoing renovation. Many of the links were not current, although when links were not working, a helpful list of suggested page links was offered.

A.P. TECHNICAL RESOURCES

www.techjobs.net

Number of job listings: Less than 250

Types of jobs: IT

Locations of jobs: Texas, Delaware, and New York

Frequency of updates: As submitted

Search by: Location

Resume database available: Yes

Employer profiles available: No

Costs for job seekers: Free

Costs for employers: Contact site

Comments: This is a relatively low-tech site that is easy to use, with an obvious personal touch.

COMPUTER JOBS

www.computerjobs.com
Number of job listings: Over 8,000
Types of jobs: Computer
Locations of jobs: United States
Frequency of updates: Hourly
Search by: Location; Keyword; Job title; Job skills; Job description; Job type; Visa sponsorship; Start-ups; Entry-level; Date posted
Resume database available: Yes
Employer profiles available: Yes
Costs for job seekers: Free
Costs for employers: Start at $200 per ad running for four weeks.
Other key features: Offers salary information; allows job seekers to save their job search results; 20 regional sites; job seekers can also have their resume matched to all available positions. The "IT Resources" section includes links to general, regional, and skill-based job search aids.

COMPUTERWORK.COM

www.computerwork.com
Number of job listings: Over 9,000
Types of jobs: Computer
Locations of jobs: United States and Canada
Frequency of updates: Daily
Search by: Keyword; Location; Job type
Resume database available: Yes
Employer profiles available: Yes
Costs for job seekers: Free
Costs for employers: $75 per job posting. Ads run for 30 days.
Other key features: A "Career Resources" section; computer training information; information on career fairs; and career news.
Comments: Ads posted to Computerwork.com also appear on 63 other sites.

Dice.com

www.dice.com
Number of job listings: Over 30,000
Types of jobs: High tech
Locations of jobs: United States
Frequency of updates: Daily
Search by: Keyword; Location; Tax term; Area code; Date posted
Resume database available: Yes
Employer profiles available: Yes
Costs for job seekers: Free
Costs for employers: Pricing starts at $225. Contact site for details.
Other key features: An e-mail notification service; relocation information; and an "Announce Availability" feature that job seekers fill out, and Dice.com then sends via e-mail to member companies.
Comments: Dice.com is one of the biggest high-tech job search sites, offering both a vast number of listings as well as a useful compilation of job search resources.

Geekfinder

www.geekfinder.com
Number of job listings: Over 29,000
Types of jobs: Computer
Locations of jobs: United States and some international
Frequency of updates: Daily
Search by: Keyword; Location; Tax term; Area code; Date posted

Resume database available: Yes
Employer profiles available: Links to employer sites within ads.
Costs for job seekers: Free
Costs for employers: Starts at $225. Contact site for details.
Other key features: "Between Geeks" articles; and "What Geeks Want" for employers.
Comments: Powered by Dice.com.

HIGH TECHNOLOGY CAREERS MAGAZINE

www.hightechcareers.com
Types of jobs: High tech
Locations of jobs: United States
Frequency of updates: Daily
Employer profiles available: Yes
Costs for job seekers: Free
Costs for employers: Vary
Other key features: Lots of career guidance and career fair information; and links to high-tech job sites.
Comments: The site offers access to a half million articles and one of the most extensive databases of high-tech employer profiles around. This site is associated with the Brass Ring Network.

IDEAS JOB NETWORK

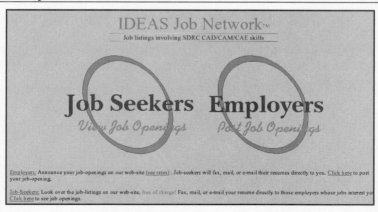

www.ideasjn.com
Types of jobs: Computer; Engineering
Locations of jobs: United States and some international
Frequency of updates: As submitted
Resume database available: No
Employer profiles available: No
Costs for job seekers: Free
Costs for employers: $100 per ad running 30 days.
Comments: All job listings involve SDRC CAD/CAE/CAM skills.

IEEE COMPUTER SOCIETY

www.computer.org/careers/index.html
Number of job listings: Less than 250
Types of jobs: Computer-related positions, often in higher education
Locations of jobs: United States and some international
Frequency of updates: Monthly
Search by: Job category; Location
Resume database available: Yes
Employer profiles available: Yes
Costs for job seekers: Free
Costs for employers: $10 per line for ads; $150 for a profile.
Other key features: Education and certification links; student activities; activity board; conference information; and a history of computing.

IT CAREERS

www.itcareers.com
Number of job listings: Over 6,000
Types of jobs: IT
Locations of jobs: United States
Frequency of updates: Daily
Search by: Keyword; Location
Resume database available: No
Employer profiles available: Yes
Costs for job seekers: Free
Costs for employers: Pricing starts at $200 per ad.
Other key features: Articles; an IT career events list; electronic newsletters; and general recruiting information.

JOBS FOR PROGRAMMERS

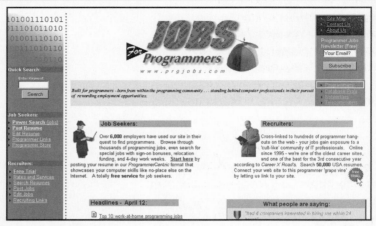

www.prgjobs.com

Types of jobs: Computer Programming

Locations of jobs: United States

Search by: Keyword; Location; Health insurance; Relocation; Educational reimbursement; Casual dress code; Sign-on bonus; Vacation time; Flexible work hours; Telecommuting jobs; 4-day workweek; Visa sponsor; Part-time; Independent contractors; Graduating college students; Entry-level applicants

Resume database available: Yes

Employer profiles available: No

Costs for job seekers: Free

Costs for employers: $249 for resume access and unlimited job postings for three months. A free 30-day trial was being offered at the time of this writing.

Other key features: Very detailed job descriptions; articles; links for programmers; and a programmers store.

Comments: By far the largest and most detailed site dedicated exclusively to computer programmers.

JOBS.INTERNET.COM

http://jobs.internet.com

Number of job listings: Over 30,000

Types of jobs: Computer

Locations of jobs: United States

Frequency of updates: Daily

Search by: Keyword; Location; Tax term; Area code; Date posted
Resume database available: Yes
Employer profiles available: No
Costs for job seekers: Free
Costs for employers: Contact site
Other key features: Skill assessment tests; rate survey; links to Dice.com resources and tools.
Comments: Powered by Dice.com.

JOB WAREHOUSE

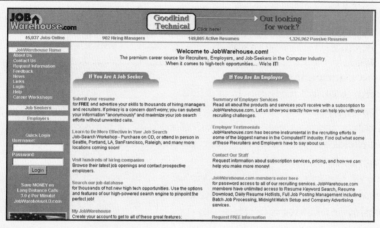

www.jobwarehouse.com
Number of job listings: Over 30,000
Types of jobs: Computer; IT
Locations of jobs: United States and some international
Frequency of updates: Daily
Search by: Keyword; Location; Job type; Employment status
Resume database available: Yes
Employer profiles available: Yes
Costs for job seekers: Free
Costs for employers: Contact site
Other key features: Resume blaster; e-mail notification service; and links to a variety of related sites.

MacTalent

www.mactalent.com

Number of job listings: Over 1,000

Types of jobs: Jobs involving Macintosh computer skills, including programming, graphic design, Web design, and desktop publishing.

Locations of jobs: United States and some international

Frequency of updates: Daily

Search by: Job category; Location; Keyword

Resume database available: Yes

Employer profiles available: No

Costs for job seekers: Free to browse jobs. Additional services are available with membership, for $29 per year.

Costs for employers: Free (although they ask that you send a contribution if you hire someone found through the site).

Other key features: A bookstore containing over 200 titles; and tips on dealing with recruiters.

Comments: This is the only site we know of designed specifically for the Mac-savvy professional.

OracleEmployment

www.oracleemployment.com

Number of job listings: Less than 250

Types of jobs: Computer, specifically programmers specializing in Oracle

Locations of jobs: United States and some international

Frequency of updates: Daily

Resume database available: No
Employer profiles available: No
Costs for job seekers: Free
Costs for employers: Free
Other key features: Links to related sites.
Comments: This is a new site, but considering the demand for Oracle professionals, look for it to grow.

SOFTMATCH.COM

www.softmatch.com
Number of job listings:
Types of jobs: High tech
Locations of jobs: United States and some international
Resume database available: Yes
Employer profiles available: No
Costs for job seekers: Free
Costs for employers: Contact site
Other key features: This site offers a Software Locator Service, matching software buyers and sellers.
Comments: Rather than list job openings, SoftMATCH lists numerous high-tech companies with links to the job openings on their respective sites.

SWIFTJOBS

www.swiftjobs.com
Number of job listings: Claims 50,000
Types of jobs: IT
Locations of jobs: United States
Frequency of updates: Daily

Search by: Keyword; Location; Date posted
Resume database available: Yes
Employer profiles available: No
Costs for job seekers: Free for basic search and resume services; Premium membership is available for $49.
Costs for employers: $199 for a one-month membership.
Other key features: Resume posting/blasting services; links to sites featuring related services, such as certification and training, salary research, and company research.
Comments: Most of the advanced services require additional fees for both employers and job seekers.

Tech-Engine

www.tech-engine.com
Number of job listings: Over 20,000 per month
Types of jobs: Computer; IT
Locations of jobs: United States
Frequency of updates: Daily
Search by: Company name; Job title; Industry; Location; Job type; Keyword
Resume database available: Yes
Employer profiles available: Yes
Costs for job seekers: Free
Costs for employers: $250 per position
Other key features: Career guide, featuring news and advice on letter writing, interviewing, resume writing, and negotiating.
Comments: Tech-Engine is one of the largest and most thorough IT job search sites on the Internet.

Techies.com

www.techies.com
Types of jobs: High tech
Locations of jobs: United States
Frequency of updates: Daily
Search by: Location; Keyword; Job category; Industry; Date posted
Resume database available: Yes
Employer profiles available: Yes
Costs for job seekers: Free
Costs for employers: Pricing starts at $295 per 60-day listing.

Other key features: Articles; each metro location has its own version of the site.

Comments: The sharp design and high-profile clientele have made this one of the fastest growing sites on the Net.

TOPSTARTUPS.COM

www.topstartups.com
Number of job listings: Less than 250
Types of jobs: Start-ups, primarily high-tech and Internet
Locations of jobs: United States
Frequency of updates: Daily
Search by: Keyword; Location
Resume database available: Yes
Employer profiles available: Yes
Costs for job seekers: Free
Costs for employers: Free for unlimited postings. For a fee, employers can be featured in the top 30 listings.
Other key features: A directory of start-up companies.

US INTERNET INDUSTRY ASSOCIATION

www.usiia.org/jobs/jobs.htm
Number of job listings: Less than 250
Types of jobs: Executive management positions in the Internet industry
Locations of jobs: United States
Frequency of updates: Every few days
Resume database available: No
Employer profiles available: No
Costs for job seekers: Free
Costs for employers: Free
Other key features: Listings of conferences and publications; and a positions wanted board for job seekers.
Comments: Positions are posted for 90 days.

Education

AASA Online

www.aasa.org/career_center/

Number of job listings: Less than 250

Types of jobs: Elementary and secondary school administrators, mostly superintendents and principals.

Locations of jobs: United States

Search by: Job category; Location; Experience; Salary; Education

Resume database available: No

Employer profiles available: No

Costs for job seekers: Free

Costs for employers: $250 for four weeks, with an extra $50 charge if the ad is submitted in any way other than through the Web site.

Other key features: E-mail notification service; sample contracts and general information important to school administrators.

Academic360.com

www.academic360.com

Types of jobs: Education

Locations of jobs: United States; Australia; Canada; United Kingdom

Search by: Location; Institution; Discipline; Job category

Resume database available: No

Employer profiles available: Yes

Costs for job seekers: Free

Other key features: Links to topical or geographic sites; access to related newsgroups; a listing of relevant associations; and links to more than 1,800 institutions of higher learning.

Comments: This is a superb collection of links that can allow job seekers to quickly surf their way into a new job.

ACADEMIC EMPLOYMENT NETWORK

www.academploy.com
Number of job listings: Less than 250
Types of jobs: Education
Locations of jobs: United States and some international
Search by: Location; Job title; Keyword; Job ID
Resume database available: Yes
Employer profiles available: Links to school Web sites in many ads
Costs for job seekers: Free to search ads; $9.95 to post a resume for six months
Costs for employers: $95 per ad running 30 days.
Other key features: Links to education-related Web sites; relocation services; and certification and development resources.
Comments: A small site that is easy to navigate and offers a good deal of useful information for the job seeker focused on an academic career.

ACADEMIC POSITION NETWORK

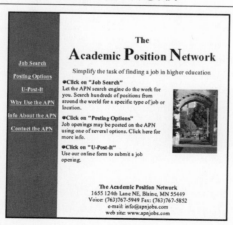

www.apnjobs.com
Number of job listings: Less than 250

Types of jobs: Education
Locations of jobs: United States and some international
Frequency of updates: Daily
Search by: Location; Discipline; Job type; Institution type
Resume database available: No
Employer profiles available: No
Costs for job seekers: Free
Costs for employers: $95 per ad running 90 days. Bulk discounts are available.
Other key features: The "U-Post-It" online job posting form for employers.
Comments: This site is lean on frills, making it easy to get down to business.

AECT PLACEMENT CENTER

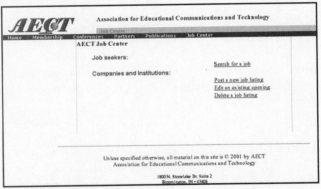

www.aect.org/job/default.htm
Number of job listings: Less than 250
Types of jobs: Education; Technical; Graduate Assistanceships
Locations of jobs: United States
Frequency of updates: Monthly
Search by: Institution; Job title; Location; Salary
Resume database available: No
Employer profiles available: No
Costs for job seekers: Free
Costs for employers: Free; ads run for 30 days.
Comments: Operated by The Association for Educational Communications & Technology. Most positions listed are with academic institutions.

Arkansas Association of Educational Administrators

www.aaea.k12.ar.us

Number of job listings: Less than 250

Types of jobs: K-12 education

Locations of jobs: Arkansas

Frequency of updates: As submitted

Search by: Job category; Job title

Resume database available: No

Employer profiles available: No

Costs for job seekers: Free

Costs for employers: You must be an AAEA member in order to post jobs.

Other key features: Links to the home pages of various education-related professional organizations and information on conferences and events.

BUCKEYE ASSOCIATION
OF SCHOOL ADMINISTRATORS

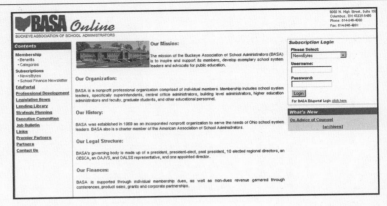

www.basa-ohio.org
Number of job listings: Less than 250
Types of jobs: Education, primarily superintendents
Locations of jobs: Ohio and some other U.S. locations
Frequency of updates: Daily
Search by: Job title; Location
Resume database available: No
Employer profiles available: No
Costs for job seekers: Free
Costs for employers: Free (members only)
Other key features: Professional development event calendar and links to associations, government agencies, and news.

THE CHRONICLE OF HIGHER
EDUCATION CAREER NETWORK

www.chronicle.com/jobs
Number of job listings: Over 3,000
Types of jobs: Academic, both faculty and non-faculty
Locations of jobs: United States and some international
Frequency of updates: Daily
Search by: Keyword; Job category; Job title; Location; Institution; Date posted
Resume database available: No

Employer profiles available: Yes, and ads include links to institution Web sites

Costs for job seekers: Basic search is free. Access to advanced features is restricted to subscribers. Online subscriptions are $75 for a year.

Costs for employers: $195 per ad running 30 days online. For inclusion in the print version too, the cost is $195 plus $1 per word.

Other key features: Subscribers can see the full text of *The Chronicle of Higher Education*, the trade newspaper for academics.

Comments: Includes listings for related positions outside of the academe including art galleries, government agencies, museums, and nonprofit organizations.

CASE

www.co-case.org

Number of job listings: Less than 250

Types of jobs: Primary and secondary education

Locations of jobs: Colorado and some other U.S. locations.

Frequency of updates: As submitted.

Search by: Keyword

Resume database available: No

Employer profiles available: No

Costs for job seekers: Free

Costs for employers: Free for members.

Other key features: Lists various local and national education links.

DAVE'S ESL CAFÉ

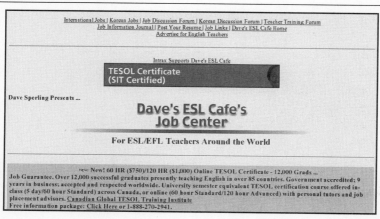

http://eslcafe.com/jobs/
Number of job listings: Over 400
Types of jobs: English as a second language teaching jobs
Locations of jobs: United States and some international
Frequency of updates: Daily
Search by: Date; Keyword
Resume database available: No
Employer profiles available: No
Costs for job seekers: Free
Costs for employers: $75 per ad running 30 days.
Other key features: Links to other ESL and EFL online resources; forums on teacher training and ESL/EFL jobs; and a Jobs Wanted board.

EDUCATION WEEK

www.edweek.org
Number of job listings: Less than 250
Types of jobs: Education
Locations of jobs: United States
Frequency of updates: Weekly
Search by: Location; Job title
Resume database available: No
Employer profiles available: No
Costs for job seekers: Free
Costs for employers: Start at $95 per column inch. Only print ads appear in the online version.
Other key features: Articles and essays relating to education issues.
Comments: This site is the online version of the newspaper *Education Week*.

HIGHEREDJOBS.COM

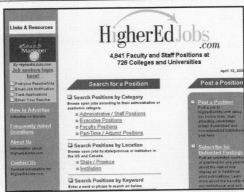

www.higheredjobs.com

Number of job listings: Over 4,500

Types of jobs: All positions in higher education

Locations of jobs: United States

Frequency of updates: Daily

Search by: Job category; Location; Keyword

Resume database available: Yes

Employer profiles available: Yes

Costs for job seekers: Free

Costs for employers: $115 per ad for three. Unlimited posting plans are also available.

Other key features: E-mail notification service; and an application tracker.

Illinois Association
of School Administrators

www.iasaedu.org

Number of job listings: Over 400

Types of jobs: Education

Locations of jobs: Illinois

Frequency of updates: Daily

Search by: Job type; Job category; Location; Grade level

Resume database available: Yes

Employer profiles available: No

Costs for job seekers: Free

Costs for employers: Based on school's enrollment.

Other key features: Links to resources and conference listings.

K12jobs.com

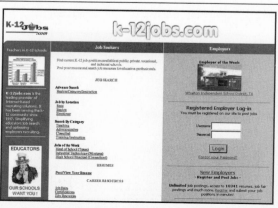

www.k12jobs.com
Types of jobs: K-12 education
Locations of jobs: United States
Frequency of updates: Daily
Search by: Location; Job category; Institution
Resume database available: Yes
Employer profiles available: Yes
Costs for job seekers: Free
Costs for employers: Prices are based on school enrollment.
Other key features: A directory of job fairs, links to education resources, and contact information for offices responsible for teacher certification.
Comments: The general information and links offered by this site make it a good stop for students and recent graduates in education.

NATIONAL ASSOCIATION FOR
COLLEGE ADMISSION COUNSELING

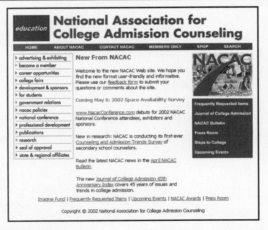

www.nacac.com
Number of job listings: Less than 250
Types of jobs: Guidance and admissions positions in higher education
Locations of jobs: United States
Frequency of updates: Every few days
Search by: Job category
Resume database available: No
Employer profiles available: No

Costs for job seekers: Free

Costs for employers: $200 for the first 200 words and $1 per word thereafter. Ads run for 30 days.

Other key features: Information on college fairs and professional development.

NATIONAL ASSOCIATION OF COLLEGE
AND UNIVERSITY BUSINESS OFFICERS

www.nacubo.org

Number of job listings: Less than 250

Types of jobs: Business Management positions at colleges and universities

Locations of jobs: United States

Frequency of updates: Monthly

Search by: Organization; Job title

Resume database available: No

Employer profiles available: No

Costs for job seekers: Free

Costs for employers: Vary by ad size. Print ads also run on the Web site. Contact site for details.

Other key features: Links to sections on professional development, publications, reports, regional associations, and a membership directory.

OHIO ASSOCIATION OF ELEMENTARY
SCHOOL ADMINISTRATORS

www.oaesa.org

Number of job listings: Less than 250

Types of jobs: Elementary school administrators, including principals, assistant principals, and superintendents.

Locations of jobs: Ohio

Frequency of updates: Daily

Search by: Job title; Location

Resume database available: No

Employer profiles available: No

Costs for job seekers: Free

Costs for employers: Contact site

Other key features: Links to other associations.

PENNSYLVANIA SCHOOL BOARDS ASSOCIATION

www.psba.org
Number of job listings: Less than 250
Types of jobs: Education
Locations of jobs: Pennsylvania
Frequency of updates: As submitted
Resume database available: No
Employer profiles available: Yes
Costs for job seekers: Free
Costs for employers: Free, but restricted to member institutions.
Other key features: Directory of Pennsylvania schools; calendar of
events with information on conferences and seminars; and links to
various sites in the education industry of Pennsylvania.

THE PRIVATE SCHOOL
EMPLOYMENT NETWORK

www.privateschooljobs.com

Types of jobs: Faculty and administrative positions with private schools

Locations of jobs: United States

Frequency of updates: Daily

Search by: Job category

Resume database available: Yes

Employer profiles available:

Costs for job seekers: Free

Costs for employers: $80 for one posting, $130 for two postings, and $175 for three postings. Please contact the site for additional pricing options. Resume access is free.

Other key features: Employers can place anonymous ads.

SCHOOL ADMINISTRATORS OF IOWA

www.sai-iowa.org

Number of job listings: Less than 250

Types of jobs: Elementary and high school education

Locations of jobs: Iowa

Frequency of updates: As submitted

Search by: Job category

Resume database available: No

Employer profiles available: No

Costs for job seekers: Free

Costs for employers: Contact site

Other key features: Links to Iowa standards for school leaders; professional development; and teacher development pages.

TEACHER JOBS

www.teacherjobs.com
Types of jobs: Education
Locations of jobs: United States
Resume database available: Yes
Employer profiles available: No
Costs for job seekers: Free to search, but a fee is required if you are hired through a contact made on the site.
Comments: Registration is required to use this site.

TeachGeorgia

www.teachgeorgia.org
Number of job listings: Over 900
Types of jobs: Education positions in public schools, primarily teachers
Locations of jobs: Georgia
Frequency of updates: Daily
Search by: School system; Job title; Discipline
Resume database available: Yes
Employer profiles available: No
Costs for job seekers: Free
Costs for employers: Contact site
Other key features: Links to job fairs; online references; and salary information.
Comments: This is likely the largest online database of teaching jobs available in Georgia.

Wisconsin Department of Public Instruction

www.wisconsin.gov/state/app/employment
Number of job listings: Over 500
Types of jobs: Education
Locations of jobs: Wisconsin
Frequency of updates: Daily
Search by: Keyword; Job category; Location
Resume database available: Yes
Employer profiles available: Yes (address only)
Costs for job seekers: Free
Costs for employers: Free
Other key features: Links to Wisconsin government employment and labor information.

Comments: This is the definitive site for anyone seeking an education position in a public institution in Wisconsin.

Engineering and Architecture

AACE INTERNATIONAL

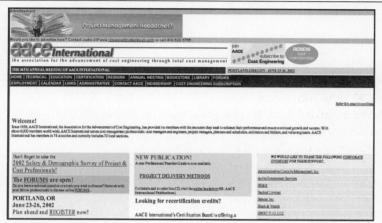

www.aacei.org

Number of job listings: Less than 250

Types of jobs: Engineering, primarily cost estimators and cost managers

Locations of jobs: United States and some international

Frequency of updates: Weekly

Resume database available: Yes

Employer profiles available: No

Costs for job seekers: Free

Costs for employers: $85 per ad per month.

Other key features: Calendar of events; library of important articles; education and certification information; and a salary survey.

Comments: Sponsored by the Association for the Advancement of Cost Engineering through Total Cost Management.

AEC JOBBANK

www.aecjobbank.com

Types of jobs: Architectural; Construction; Engineering; Real estate

Locations of jobs: United States

Frequency of updates: Daily

Search by: Job title; Job category; Job type; Employee type; Education; Experience; Travel; Location; Salary

Resume database available: Yes

Employer profiles available: Yes

Costs for job seekers: Free

Costs for employers: Pricing starts at $75 for a single ad.

Other key features: This site's design allows for a quickly narrowed search.

Comments: Registration is required to use this site.

AMERICAN INSTITUTE
OF CHEMICAL ENGINEERS

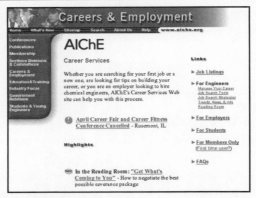

www.aiche.org/careerservices/

Number of job listings: Less than 250

Types of jobs: Chemical Engineering

Locations of jobs: United States

Frequency of updates: Daily

Search by: Keyword; Company name; SIC code

Resume database available: Yes

Employer profiles available: No

Costs for job seekers: Free

Costs for employers: $3.00 per word.

Other key features: Job search resources; industry news; and career fair information.

THE AMERICAN SOCIETY FOR
ENGINEERING EDUCATION

www.asee.org
Number of job listings: Less than 250
Types of jobs: Faculty positions with college engineering departments
Locations of jobs: United States
Frequency of updates: Daily (monthly for nonmembers)
Resume database available: No
Employer profiles available: No
Costs for job seekers: Free (many services require ASEE membership)
Costs for employers: $3.75 per word by e-mail, $4.00 per word if mailed or faxed.
Comments: ASEE members can view classified ads from both current and past issues. Nonmembers can only view ads from the current month. Basic, individual membership is $99 per year, which includes full online privileges and *ASEE Prism*, the society's printed publication. Student memberships are $20 per year.

AMERICAN SOCIETY
OF CIVIL ENGINEERS

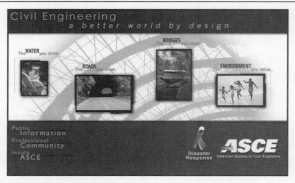

www.asce.org/careers/index.cfm
Types of jobs: Civil engineering
Locations of jobs: United States
Frequency of updates: Weekly
Search by: Job title; Keyword; Location
Resume database available: No
Employer profiles available: No

Costs for job seekers: Free
Costs for employers: $1.00 per word, with a $50.00 minimum.
Other key features: Information on conferences, distance learning, on-site training, and seminars.

AMERICAN SOCIETY
OF LANDSCAPE ARCHITECTS

www.asla.org
Number of job listings: Less than 250
Types of jobs: Landscape architecture
Locations of jobs: United States
Frequency of updates: Daily
Resume database available: Yes
Employer profiles available: No
Costs for job seekers: Free to search job listings. Resume posting costs $10 for ASLA members, $100 for nonmembers.
Costs for employers: $200 per ad running two months for ASLA members, $450 for nonmembers.
Other key features: Tons of industry-related information; links to information on all aspects of landscape architecture. Jobs are listed by date.
Comments: Membership rates vary by location and employment status. Membership includes a subscription to *Landscape Architecture* magazine, the *LAND* newsletter, and full online access.

The daVinci Project

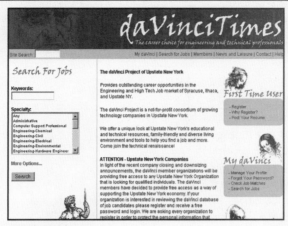

www.davincitimes.com

Number of job listings: Less than 250

Types of jobs: Engineering

Locations of jobs: Upstate New York

Frequency of updates: Daily

Search by: Keyword; Job category; Date posted; Job type; Education; Experience; Degree of travel; Location; Salary

Resume database available: Yes

Employer profiles available: Yes

Costs for job seekers: Free

Costs for employers: A five-job posting packet is $550. Postings run for 60 days.

Other key features: Lots of information on how great a place Upstate New York is to live.

Comments: The daVinci Project is a consortium of Upstate New York engineering firms and institutions that are working together to attract engineering talent to the Upstate New York area. The site's sole purpose is recruiting job seekers, not to turn a profit.

Engineeringjobs.com

www.engineeringjobs.com

Types of jobs: Engineering

Locations of jobs: United States

Search by: Headhunter

Resume database available: No

Employer profiles available: No
Costs for job seekers: Free
Costs for employers: Free
Comments: Rather than list jobs, this site features links to headhunters that feature job opportunities on their Web sites.

ENGINEERJOBS.COM

www.engineerjobs.com
Number of job listings: Over 700
Types of jobs: Engineering
Locations of jobs: United States
Frequency of updates: Daily
Search by: Location; Keyword; Company name; Job title
Resume database available: Yes
Employer profiles available: No
Costs for job seekers: Free
Costs for employers: $30 per ad running 60 days, $600 per 100 listings for two months, or $3,000 per 100 listings each month for one year. Other advertising packages are available. Resume access is included in payment for job listings. When we last checked, the site was offering 15 job listings free.
Other key features: An e-mail notification service; and links to other engineering and technical sites.
Comments: This is one of the more popular and resourceful sites related to engineering jobs, and it has expanded nationwide since our last review.

NATIONAL SOCIETY
OF PROFESSIONAL ENGINEERS

www.nspe.org/em-home.asp
Number of job listings: Over 300
Types of jobs: Engineering
Locations of jobs: United States
Search by: Location; Company name; Industry sector; Job category; Keyword
Resume database available: Yes
Employer profiles available: No
Costs for job seekers: Free

Costs for employers: $150 per 60-day posting. Additional packages are available.

Comments: This site appears to be offering a far greater number of job listings since our last review, indicating strong success and growth.

Environmental

ENVIRONMENTAL CAREER

OPPORTUNITIES

www.ecojobs.com
Number of job listings: Over 500
Types of jobs: Environmental
Locations of jobs: United States
Frequency of updates: Biweekly
Search by: Job category
Resume database available: No
Employer profiles available: No
Costs for job seekers: Free; however, to view all the jobs you must have a subscription to the *Environmental Career Opportunities* newsletter.
Costs for employers: $89 per ad for the first week's issue, $69 per ad for each week thereafter. Ads run in both print and online versions.

THE ENVIRONMENTAL

CAREERS CENTER

www.environmentalcareer.com
Number of job listings: Less than 250
Types of jobs: Environmental
Locations of jobs: United States
Frequency of updates: Weekly
Resume database available: No
Employer profiles available: No
Costs for job seekers: Free
Costs for employers: $79 per ad running 30 days, $39 for nonprofits. Bulk rates are also available.
Other key features: Links to salary surveys, environmental engineer staffing agencies, and professional societies.
Comments: The Environmental Career Center also offers a monthly publication titled *National Environment Report*, which lists between 600 and 1,200 jobs per month and provides career and networking advice and information. Subscription rates start at $19 for three issues.

Texas Parks & Wildlife

www.tpwd.state.tx.us/involved/jobvac/job.htm
Number of job listings: Less than 250
Types of jobs: Jobs with parks and historic sites.
Locations of jobs: Texas
Frequency of updates: Daily
Search by: Job title; Job category; Location; Division
Resume database available: No
Employer profiles available: No
Costs for job seekers: Free
Other key features: State of Texas job application available for download.

Water Environment Web

www.wef.org
Types of jobs: Water quality professionals
Locations of jobs: United States
Frequency of updates: Every few days
Resume database available: Yes
Employer profiles available: No
Costs for job seekers: Free to members

Costs for employers: $225 for an experienced level job posting; $125 for an entry-level job posting; $25 for an internship job posting. All ads run 30 days.

Comments: Membership costs vary by type of membership requested. Contact site for complete details

Government

THE BLUE LINE

www.theblueline.com
Number of job listings: Less than 250
Types of jobs: Law enforcement
Locations of jobs: United States
Frequency of updates: Monthly
Resume database available: No
Employer profiles available: No
Costs for job seekers: $39.95 for a six-month subsricption.
Costs for employers: $199 for the featured department plan
Other key features: Links to other law enforcement Web sites.

CORPORATE GRAY ONLINE

www.bluetogray.com
Number of job listings: 300
Types of jobs: All
Locations of jobs: United States
Frequency of updates:
Search by: Keyword; Location; Job category

Resume database available: Yes
Employer profiles available: Yes
Costs for job seekers: Free
Costs for employers: Free if you self-post; $200 per month if you FTP them to the site.
Other key features: Links to career resources designed for people leaving the military.

FEDERAL JOBS CENTRAL

www.fedjobs.com
Number of job listings: Over 17,000
Types of jobs: Federal government
Locations of jobs: United States
Frequency of updates: Daily
Search by: Federal Job Series; Salary; Location; Federal/Nonfederal opportunities
Resume database available: No
Employer profiles available: No
Costs for job seekers: $19.97 per month, or $49 for three months for unlimited use.
Costs for employers: Contact site
Other key features: A calendar of events; career tips; information on federal agencies.
Comments: This site gathers its job openings through its own research. Even with meticulous tending, such a large database would tend to have outdated information. Considering its size, the price may be worth it to job seekers serious about working for the

federal government; for those unsure, you can sample the listing without the full details for free.

FEDERAL JOBS DIGEST

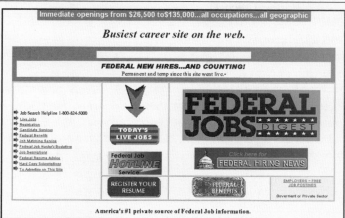

Immediate openings from $26,500 to$135,000...all occupations...all geographic

Busiest career site on the web.

FEDERAL NEW HIRES...AND COUNTING!
Permanent and temp since this site went live.•

Job Search Helpline 1-800-824-5000
Live Jobs
Registration
Candidate Services
Federal Benefits
Job Matching Service
Federal Job Hunter's Bookstore
Job Descriptions
Federal Resume Advice
Hard Copy Subscriptions
To Advertise on This Site

TODAY'S LIVE JOBS

FEDERAL JOBS DIGEST ★★★★★

Federal Job HOTLINE Service

Click here for FEDERAL HIRING NEWS

REGISTER YOUR RESUME

FEDERAL BENEFITS

EMPLOYERS – FREE JOB POSTINGS
Government or Private Sector

America's #1 private source of Federal Job information.

www.jobsfed.com
Number of job listings: Over 17,000
Types of jobs: Government
Locations of jobs: United States
Frequency of updates: Daily
Search by: Job category
Resume database available: Yes
Employer profiles available: No
Costs for job seekers: Free if you register your resume.
Costs for employers: Free for regular listing; 20 cents per click through for hyperlinked listing.
Other key features: A detailed resume posting area; a listing of the most recent job postings; a jobs bulletin board; listing of hotlines; a job matching service; information on federal benefits; and anonymous resumes.
Comments: This claims to be the busiest career site on the Web, with over 2.5 million new federal hires since 1996 (at the time of this writing).

FedWorld Federal Jobs

www.fedworld.gov/jobs/jobsearch.html
Types of jobs: All
Locations of jobs: United States
Frequency of updates: Daily
Search by: Keyword; Location
Resume database available: No
Employer profiles available: No
Costs for job seekers: Free
Other key features: Includes links to numerous other sites and access to various government databases, using FirstGov, where you can find archival information on business, the environment, and many other subjects. You can also find and order information from the U.S. government.

Law Enforcement
Recruiting Directory

www.officer.com/recruiting/index.htm
Types of jobs: Law enforcement
Locations of jobs: United States and some international
Costs for job seekers: Free
Comments: This site doesn't list job openings, but rather provides links to law enforcement sites that do list jobs and related information.

USA Jobs

www.usajobs.opm.gov

Types of jobs: All

Locations of jobs: United States

Frequency of updates: Daily

Search by: Job type; Keyword; Experience

Resume database available: Yes

Employer profiles available: No

Costs for job seekers: Free

Other key features: Online career transition assistance provided by the U.S. Department of Labor and various other government information sources.

Comments: Operated by the U.S. Office of Personnel Management, USA Jobs is the government's official site for jobs and employment information. It contains information on: applying for federal jobs, federal salary and benefits, student employment, and more. Job listings are neatly divided into professional, clerical and technical, trades and labor, senior executive, entry-level, worker-trainee, and summer positions.

Health Care

ALLIED HEALTH OPPORTUNITIES

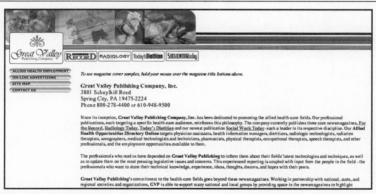

www.gvpub.com

Number of job listings: Less than 250

Types of jobs: Allied health professionals

Locations of jobs: United States

Frequency of updates: Weekly

Search by: Job category; Location; Keyword

Resume database available: No

Employer profiles available:

Costs for job seekers: Free

Costs for employers: The basic cost is $50 per month per ad, with a variety of packages available.

Comments: Sponsored by Great Valley Publishing Company, publisher of the trade journals *Social Work Today*, *For the Record*, and *Today's Dietician*.

THE AMERICAN ASSOCIATION FOR CLINICAL CHEMISTRY

www.aacc.org/employment

Number of job listings: Less than 250

Types of jobs: Clinical laboratory

Locations of jobs: United States

Frequency of updates: Daily

Search by: Location; Job category; Salary; Region; Degree

Resume database available: No

Employer profiles available: No

Costs for job seekers: Free

Costs for employers: Free

Other key features: Links for continuing education; distance learning; meetings and audioconferences; and the AACC listserv program.

AMERICA'S HEALTH CARE SOURCE

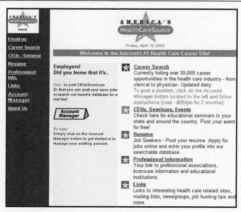

www.healthcaresource.com

Number of job listings: Over 20,000

Types of jobs: Health care

Locations of jobs: United States
Frequency of updates: Daily
Search by: Job category; Facility name; Location
Resume database available: Yes
Employer profiles available: Direct links to employer sites from ads.
Costs for job seekers: Free
Costs for employers: $95 per ad running two months.
Other key features: Links to health care industry sites, career resources, and professional associations.
Comments: This site was rated the best job hunting site by *Hospitals and Health Networks*, a publication of the American Hospital Association.

HEALTH CAREER WEB

www.healthcareerweb.com
Types of jobs: Health care
Locations of jobs: United States
Frequency of updates: Daily
Search by: Job category; Keyword; Location
Resume database available: Yes
Employer profiles available: Yes
Costs for job seekers: Free
Costs for employers: A basic job listing is free. Please contact the site for details on pricing options for more advanced packages, including costs to access resumes.
Other key features: Instant interview; career articles and advice; an e-mail notification service; and links to career books.
Comments: Powered by CareerWeb.

HEALTH CARE JOBS ONLINE

www.hcjobsonline.com
Number of job listings: Less than 250
Types of jobs: Health care
Locations of jobs: United States
Frequency of updates: As submitted.
Search by: Job category; Keyword
Resume database available: No
Employer profiles available: Direct links to employer Web sites from ads.

Costs for job seekers: Free

Costs for employers: $50 per ad running one month.

Other key features: Links to health care and career related sites; and salary and relocation information.

HEALTH CARE RECRUITMENT ONLINE

www.healthcarerecruitment.com

Number of job listings: Over 9,000

Types of jobs: Health care

Locations of jobs: United States

Frequency of updates: Daily

Search by: Job category; Location

Resume database available: No

Employer profiles available: Yes

Costs for job seekers: Free

Costs for employers: Contact site

Other key features: Online registration for direct contact with employers.

HEALTHOPPS

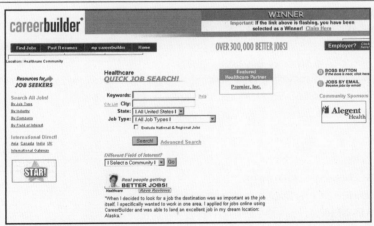

www.healthopps.com

Number of job listings: Over 5,000

Types of jobs: Health care

Locations of jobs: United States and some international

Frequency of updates: Daily

Search by: Keyword; Location; Job type; Date posted; Degree; Salary; Employment type; Position type; Company type
Resume database available: Yes
Employer profiles available: Yes
Costs for job seekers: Free
Costs for employers: Rates vary, depending on the size of your organization. Contact site for details.
Other key features: Resource page, including information on career assessment, resume distribution, work visas, relocation, and legal concerns.
Comments: This site has merged with the Healthcare Community of Headhunter.net, part of the CareerBuilder network of sites.

MEDHUNTERS
www.medhunters.com
Number of job listings: Over 7,000
Types of jobs: Health care
Locations of jobs: United States and some international
Frequency of updates: Daily
Search by: Job category
Resume database available: Yes
Employer profiles available: Yes
Costs for job seekers: Free
Costs for employers: A variety of packages are available. Contact site for details.
Other key features: Relocation information; licensing information; and links to various career resources.

MEDICAL DEVICE LINK
www.devicelink.com/career
Number of job listings: Over 250
Types of jobs: Medical devices
Locations of jobs: United States
Frequency of updates: Daily
Search by: Keyword
Resume database available: Yes
Employer profiles available: Yes
Costs for job seekers: Free
Costs for employers: Contact site

Other key features: Articles; discussion forums; salary estimator; and research and industry links.

Comments: Registration is required to view ad contents and post resumes.

MEDZILLA

www.medzilla.com

Types of jobs: Biotechnology; Health care; Science

Locations of jobs: United States

Frequency of updates: Daily

Search by: Keyword; Company name; Location

Resume database available: Yes

Employer profiles available: No

Costs for job seekers: Free

Costs for employers: Start at $95 per ad running one month. Contact site for pricing on resume access and multiple job listings.

Other key features: Forums; articles; and links related to the biotech industry.

Comments: A good resource for job seekers in health care and related fields. Some listings include extensive employer descriptions, and an area set up to automatically e-mail the employer.

NURSING SPECTRUM

CAREER FITNESS ONLINE

www.nursingspectrum.com

Number of job listings: Over 2,000

Types of jobs: Nursing
Locations of jobs: United States
Frequency of updates: As submitted.
Search by: Job category; Location; Keyword
Resume database available: No
Employer profiles available: Yes
Costs for job seekers: Free
Costs for employers: $150 per ad running two weeks.
Other key features: A schedule of nationwide nursing events; a chat area; nursing forum; resources including nursing books, health care policy information, educational resources; and an e-mail notification service. Some ads offer an instant interview option.

PHYSICIANS EMPLOYMENT

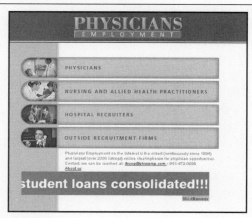

www.physemp.com
Number of job listings: Over 2,000
Types of jobs: Health care
Locations of jobs: United States
Frequency of updates: As submitted.
Search by: Job category
Resume database available: No
Employer profiles available: Direct links to employer sites in ads.
Costs for job seekers: Free
Costs for employers: Contact site for pricing information.
Comments: Before being able to view just about any information, the site asks for a basic profile.

Hotels and Restaurants

Casino Careers Online

www.casinocareers.com

Number of job listings: Less than 250

Types of jobs: All types of jobs with casinos

Locations of jobs: United States

Frequency of updates: Daily

Search by: Job category

Resume database available: Yes

Employer profiles available: No

Costs for job seekers: Free

Costs for employers: For $400, qualified employers receive a single job opening slot and access to resumes. Slots can be changed to reflect a new job opening. Employers with fewer than 1,000 employees can get a full annual membership for $5,000 (includes unlimited job posting and resume access). Additional packages are also available.

Other key features: "Hot News" links to various articles concerning gaming careers. The site also includes a few links that may be helpful to anyone seeking a career in the gaming/hospitality industry.

Escoffier Online

www.escoffier.com/nonscape/employ.shtml

Number of job listings: Less than 250

Types of jobs: Hospitality

Locations of jobs: United States
Frequency of updates: Daily
Search by: Job category
Resume database available: No
Employer profiles available: No
Costs for job seekers: Free to search ads. $49.95 per ad per month for "positions sought" section.
Costs for employers: $49.95 per ad running one month, or $100 per month for unlimited postings. The positions sought section can be searched for free. There is a $15 surcharge on ad copy not submitted through online posting.
Other key features: The Career Center includes links to resume and interview tips and advice.

StarChefs

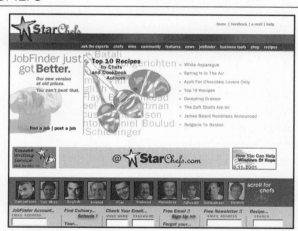

www.starchefs.com
Number of job listings: Less than 250
Types of jobs: Hotel/Restaurant, primarily chefs and cooks, but some management and food service positions were offered.
Locations of jobs: United States and some international
Frequency of updates: Daily
Search by: Keyword; Company name; Job category; Location
Resume database available: Yes
Employer profiles available: Yes
Costs for job seekers: Free
Costs for employers: A single 30-day job posting is $99.

Other key features: Free newsletter; recipes; free e-mail account; and a variety of cooking and food links.

Comments: Most highly specialized positions are only offered in one or two locations in the country. Sous chefs will have the most luck on this site. The site works in conjunction with Culinaryjobfinder.com.

Human Resources/Recruiting

HR WORLD

www.hrworld.com
Number of job listings: Less than 250
Types of jobs: Human resources
Locations of jobs: United States
Frequency of updates: Daily
Search by: Job category; Job type
Resume database available: Yes
Employer profiles available: No
Costs for job seekers: Free
Costs for employers: Contact site

Other key features: Forums; information on human resources products and services; access to human resources articles and publications; and links to worldwide human resources sites.

Comments: Much of the information is only accessible to registered users (registration is free). A must for all HR professionals to check out—both those seeking employment and those seeking employees.

HR.com

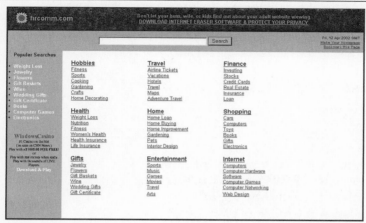

www.hr.com

Number of job listings: Over 2,000

Types of jobs: Human resources and recruiting

Locations of jobs: United States

Frequency of updates: Daily

Search by: Industry; Location; Keyword; Job type

Resume database available: Yes

Employer profiles available: Yes

Costs for job seekers: Free

Costs for employers: $150 for a 30-day job posting; $200 per month for resume access.

Other key features: Articles; event calendar; and links to a wide variety of HR-related services and sites.

Comments: HR.com is a highly recommended site for people in the human resources industry.

IHRIM

http://ihr.hrdpt.com

Number of job listings: Less than 250

Types of jobs: Human resources information management

Locations of jobs: United States

Frequency of updates: Every few days

Search by: Keyword

Resume database available: Yes

Employer profiles available: No

Costs for job seekers: Free

Costs for employers: Start at $200 per ad running 30 days. Longer ads and bulk posting packages are available.

Other key features: Lots of career information and industry news for those in the human resources field.

INTERNATIONAL FOUNDATION

OF EMPLOYEE BENEFIT PLANS

www.ifebp.org/jobs

Number of job listings: Less than 250

Types of jobs: Human resources

Locations of jobs: United States

Frequency of updates: Daily

Search by: Date posted; Location; Job title; Company name

Resume database available: Yes

Employer profiles available: No

Costs for job seekers: Free; $30 to post a resume for 180 days (free for members of the International Foundation).

Costs for employers: $185 per ad running 60 days ($160 for members of the International Foundation). Renewals are available at a reduced rate.

Other key features: Links to various professional organizations; and an archive of articles of interest to HR professionals.

JOBS 4 HR

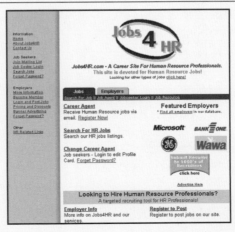

www.jobs4hr.com
Number of job listings: Less than 250
Types of jobs: Human resources
Locations of jobs: United States
Frequency of updates: Daily
Search by: Company name; Keyword; Location; Job category
Resume database available: Yes (in the form of profiles)
Employer profiles available: No
Costs for job seekers: Free
Costs for employers: $100 for one ad, $450 for five ads, $750 for 10 ads, $1,000 for unlimited postings for three months, or $2,500 for unlimited postings for one year.
Other key features: E-mail notification service; a mailing list connecting job seekers and employers; and links to other HR sites.
Comments: Sponsors include Microsoft, General Electric, and Bank One. Operated by Recruiters Network.

SOCIETY FOR HUMAN
RESOURCE MANAGEMENT

www.shrm.org/jobs
Types of jobs: Human resources professionals
Locations of jobs: United States
Frequency of updates: Daily
Search by: Date posted; Location; Keyword
Resume database available: No
Employer profiles available: No

Costs for job seekers: Free

Costs for employers: $20 per line for an ad running one month.

Other key features: E-mail job alert; weekly articles; and a variety of HR-related links and information pages.

Comments: It's often the HR professional's job to find employees, so naturally a site dedicated to recruiting HR staff would be detailed, organized, and above all, crammed full of listings that can be organized in multiple convenient lists for the job seeker's browsing pleasure. Some of the services are available only to SHRM members.

WORLD AT WORK

www.worldatwork.org

Number of job listings: Less than 250

Types of jobs: Human resources

Locations of jobs: United States

Frequency of updates: Daily

Search by: Location; Job title; Keyword

Resume database available: No

Employer profiles available: No

Costs for job seekers: Free to ACA members

Costs for employers: $175 per ad (up to 125 words) running six weeks. For ads over 125 words, the cost is $1 per additional word. Blind ads are also available for an extra $25.

Other key features: Positions wanted section for job seekers.

Comments: Membership to the ACA is $160 per year, and offers other services, including a directory of members.

Insurance

ACTUARY.COM

www.actuary.com

Number of job listings: Less than 250

Types of jobs: Insurance

Locations of jobs: United States

Frequency of updates: Daily

Search by: Job category; Location; Keyword

Resume database available: No

Employer profiles available: No

Costs for job seekers: Free

Costs for employers: $200 per posting for 60 days.

Other key features: Discussion groups; exam information; jokes; directory of recruiting firms; regulatory information; and much more.

Comments: Actuary.com is perhaps the largest single online resource of insurance-related information and resources available.

INSURANCE NATIONAL SEARCH

www.insurancerecruiters.com

Number of job listings: Less than 250

Types of jobs: Insurance

Locations of jobs: United States

Frequency of updates: Daily

Search by: Department; Line of business; Location; Date posted; Salary; Keyword

Resume database available: No

Employer profiles available: Yes (recruiters only)

Costs for job seekers: Free

Costs for employers: Contact site

Comments: This site is a nationwide network of insurance recruiting firms.

Legal

EMPLAWYERNET

www.emplawyernet.com

Number of job listings: Over 4,000

Types of jobs: Legal

Locations of jobs: United States and some international
Frequency of updates:
Search by:
Resume database available: Yes
Employer profiles available:
Costs for job seekers: Basic membership is free and allows job seekers to post a resume, but only gives limited access to jobs. $59.95 annual fee and $14.95 per month for Premier Membership, which includes full access to the job listings and resume services.
Costs for employers: $150 per standard job posting.
Other key features: An e-mail notification system for Premier Members; Employment Connection, allowing job seekers to make anonymous hiring inquiries.

LAW JOBS

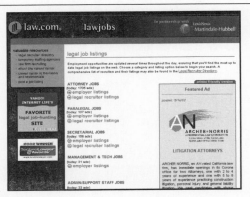

www.lawjobs.com
Number of job listings: Over 1,500
Types of jobs: Legal
Locations of jobs: United States
Frequency of updates: As submitted
Search by: Job category; Location; Practice area
Resume database available: No
Employer profiles available: Yes
Costs for job seekers: Free
Costs for employers: Contact site
Other key features: List of recruiters; e-mail service allows job seekers to easily send postings to friends and colleagues; and links to temporary agencies, regional classified ads, and related news.

THE LEGAL EMPLOYMENT
SEARCH SITE

www.legalemploy.com
Types of jobs: Legal
Locations of jobs: United States
Search by: None
Comments: This site lists links to sites covering legal employment, law school career service offices, general employment, online resume posting, and other general sites that may be of value to individuals in the legal field.

RIGHT OF WAY

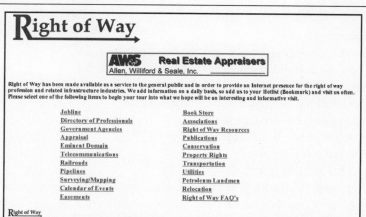

www.rightofway.com/jobline.html
Number of job listings: Less than 250
Types of jobs: Right of way and property rights professionals
Locations of jobs: United States
Resume database available: Yes (in the form of short applicant profiles)
Employer profiles available: No
Costs for job seekers: Free
Costs for employers: Free
Other key features: Directories of professionals and government agencies; online bookstore; associations; a calendar of events; and sections devoted to information relevant to legal matters.

Mining/Gas/Petroleum

OIL AND GAS ONLINE

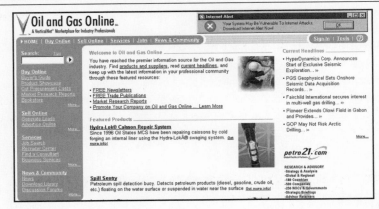

www.oillink.com
Types of jobs: Energy-related; Gas; Mining; Petroleum
Locations of jobs: United States
Frequency of updates: Daily
Search by: Keyword; Location; Date posted
Resume database available: Yes
Employer profiles available: Yes
Costs for job seekers: Free
Costs for employers: $100 for 30 days
Other key features: Resume software; online bookstore; "Career Club" career enhancement center; online tutorials; and a free newsletter.

Printing and Publishing

CALIFORNIA JOURNALISM JOB BANK

www.csne.org
Number of job listings: Less than 250
Types of jobs: Journalism
Locations of jobs: United States
Frequency of updates: Daily
Resume database available: No
Employer profiles available: No
Costs for job seekers: Free

Costs for employers: Free for CSNE members; $100 for papers in California and Nevada; and $150 for all other papers.

Other key features: The "Journalist's Toolbox" contains links to a variety of information sources from government sites to meta-lists of value.

Comments: Many of the job listings are with smaller newspapers.

MEDIABISTRO.COM

www.mediabistro.com

Number of job listings: Less than 250

Types of jobs: Publishing/Media

Locations of jobs: United States

Frequency of updates: Daily

Search by: Industry; Location; Keyword

Resume database available: Yes

Employer profiles available: No

Costs for job seekers: Free

Costs for employers: $199 per ad, or $275 for an ad covering multiple positions.

Other key features: Bulletin board; events list; articles; interviews; reviews; and advice.

Comments: There is a 10-day money back guarantee on job ads. For anyone serious about the publishing industry, mediabistro.com offers some great opportunities at some of the industry's most reputable companies. Free registration is required for some features, and includes additional freebies, such as newsletters, special offers, and invitations to cocktail parties.

NEWSLINK

http://newslink.org
Number of job listings: Less than 250
Types of jobs: Publishing
Locations of jobs: United States and international
Frequency of updates: Daily
Search by: Ad type; Industry; Experience; Education; Opening type; Position; Location; Salary; Specialty; Environment; Keyword; Date posted
Resume database available: Yes
Employer profiles available: No
Costs for job seekers: Free
Costs for employers: $65 per ad running five weeks. Resumes may be accessed free of charge.
Other key features: Over 10,000 links to newspapers, magazines, and other media resources; related news articles; an e-mail notification service; and a research section.
Comments: This site was recently spun off from the online version of *American Journalism Review*.

WRITERS WRITE

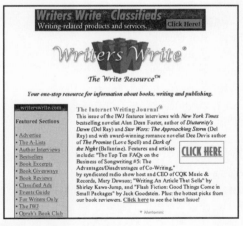

www.writerswrite.com
Number of job listings: Less than 250
Types of jobs: Editing; Writing
Locations of jobs: United States
Frequency of updates: Daily

Search by: Job type; Position; Industry

Resume database available: Yes, in the form of "Writers On Call," a short profile with contact information.

Employer profiles available: Yes

Costs for job seekers: Free to search jobs; $45 for eight weeks on "Writers On Call," or $85 for 16 weeks.

Costs for employers: $45 per ad running five weeks, $85 for 10 weeks.

Other key features: Author interviews; book excerpts; book reviews; book giveaways; an online bookstore; and many other writing and publishing-related links.

Comments: Primarily freelance jobs.

Retail

FASHION CAREER CENTER

www.fashioncareercenter.com

Number of job listings: Less than 250

Types of jobs: Fashion

Locations of jobs: United States

Frequency of updates: Daily

Search by: Keyword; Location

Resume database available: Yes

Employer profiles available: No

Costs for job seekers: Free

Costs for employers: For nonmembers, $60 per ad running 60 days and $99 to view resumes for one month. Members can post jobs and access resumes for free.

Other key features: The Career Services link lists the site's fee-based services including resume distribution, portfolio assistance, and executive search services. The site also lists links to every major college and university worldwide that offers a fashion program. The Career Advice link gives helpful information about the fashion industry.

Comments: Full membership packages start at $845 for six months.

MONSTER RETAIL

http://retail.monster.com
Number of job listings: Over 5,000
Types of jobs: Retail and wholesale
Locations of jobs: United States
Frequency of updates: Daily
Search by: Location; Keyword
Resume database available: Yes
Employer profiles available: Yes
Costs for job seekers: Free
Costs for employers: Contact site
Other key features: Articles; salary calculator; resume center; message boards; and more.
Comments: This is the retail section of Monster.com, devoted entirely to the retail and wholesale industry.

RETAIL JOBNET

www.retailjobnet.com
Types of jobs: Retail
Locations of jobs: United States and Canada
Search by: Location; Job category; Job title
Resume database available: Yes
Employer profiles available: No
Costs for job seekers: Free
Costs for employers: Starts at $139 per ad running one month. Resumes may be accessed at the rate of $99 per month or $599 per year.
Other key features: Links to other retail sites.

Transportation

INTERNATIONAL SEAFARERS EXCHANGE

www.jobxchange.com
Types of jobs: Cruise ship and maritime positions

Locations of jobs: United States and some international

Search by: Department

Resume database available: Yes

Costs for job seekers: $39 to view the "CrewXchange" job links; $30 to post a resume for six months.

Costs for employers: $125 per employment link. Other services are offered for additional fees.

Other key features: The WorkAbroad link offers information on 325 types of on-board positions including salary, benefits, and experience and skills required; and helpful information on landing a seafaring job and making the transition to life at sea.

Comments: Rather than listing jobs, this site indexes links to the job pages of various maritime companies including cruise lines and commercial vessels. The cost may be a factor, but the site does offer enough free information and free sampling options to make it definitely worth a look.

1-800-DRIVERS

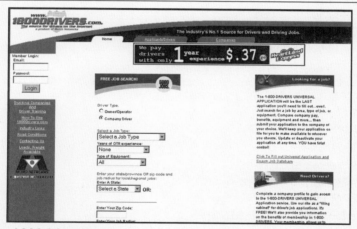

www.1800drivers.com

Types of jobs: Trucking

Locations of jobs: United States and some international

Frequency of updates:

Search by: Driver type; Job type; Experience; Equipment type; Location; Pet policy; Rider policy; Benefits; Dedicated driver manager; Satellite communication; Home time

Resume database available: Yes, in the form of an online application

Employer profiles available: Yes

Costs for job seekers: Free
Costs for employers: Contact site
Other key features: Offers information on road conditions, construction notices, and trucking regulations for most major highways in the United States; online application forms and links to employer Web sites; and various other trucking-related sites.
Comments: Whether looking for the long hauls or local delivery, truckers should check out this stop for their future employment needs.

Utilities

PLATTS GLOBAL ENERGY

www.platts.com/engineering/index.shtml
Number of job listings: Less than 250
Types of jobs: Electric power and energy industries
Locations of jobs: United States and some international
Frequency of updates: Weekly
Resume database available: No
Employer profiles available: No
Costs for job seekers: Free
Costs for employers: Contact site
Other key features: Links to other energy-related sites and articles relating to power and electric utilities.
Comments: This site provides access to job listings from the Platts Job Bank, *Power* magazine, and *Electrical World T & D.*

WATER ONLINE

www.wateronline.com
Number of job listings: Over 1,400
Types of jobs: Water/Wastewater
Locations of jobs: United States
Frequency of updates: Daily
Search by: Keyword; Location; Job title; Date posted; Job category
Resume database available: Yes
Employer profiles available: Yes
Costs for job seekers: Free
Costs for employers: Contact site
Other key features: Industry news; product information; and an employer spotlight all geared toward water professionals and employers.
Comments: Water Online is affiliated with Dice.com.

CHAPTER SIX

RESEARCHING COMPANIES ONLINE

Investigating potential employers is critical to the job hunting process. Whether you are researching companies to target in your job search, or trying to educate yourself about a potential employer's background, it is essential to have thorough, up-to-date information about your target companies. Using the World Wide Web is one of the fastest, easiest, and most effective ways to research companies. Employer profiles are popping up on an increasing number of job sites, and virtually every company has their own Web site.

Creating Your Target List of Companies

Advance research is essential to any job hunt. Otherwise, you could waste time sending resumes to companies that don't hire for your position, or that don't have the type of atmosphere you're looking for (in terms of company size, for example). One of the first steps in any job hunt is deciding which companies are likely to hire someone with your skills and experience and which ones you would like to work for. The easiest way to do this is to take a few minutes to think about what you want to do, and in what type of atmosphere you'd like to do it.

Decide what type of company you want to work for. Look at geographical location, product line, company size, and customer type (such as industrial or consumer). Try to figure out at which companies your skills can best be put to use, and in what type of environment you'll most likely be able to thrive.

Researching Commercial Online Services

Services like America Online and CompuServe are gold mines of valuable information for job seekers. Job hunters can find detailed information that helps them target potential employers or prepare for job interviews. Costs of the services will vary. Most databases on CompuServe charge a search fee in addition to the CompuServe subscription charges. America Online, on the other hand, has a smaller selection of business resources, but the information is available free of charge. Many job seekers may find that they don't really need the in-depth financial information that many of the more expensive databases like CompuServe provide.

Researching Employers Online

The type of company information you can find online varies greatly from the telephone book style of the "SuperPages" to the detailed financial information found in Dun & Bradstreet's Business Reports. Some information comes in the form of employer databases on CD-ROMs where you can conduct searches according to criteria such as geographic location and industry. Many Web sites simply contain a list of companies, with links to each company's home page. General job hunting sites, like Monster.com, include employer profiles of those companies with job listings at the site (check out the listings in Chapters Three, Four, and Five to find out which sites offer company profiles). CareerCity.com lists profiles of tens of thousands of U.S. companies with hyperlinks. Other databases, both on the Web and through commercial online services, contain much more in-depth information regarding a company's history, financial standing, or its products and services.

If you have a relatively short list of target companies you would like to learn more about, another option is to simply check out each company's home page on the Web. Since most sites are geared toward consumers, most individual company Web sites include detailed information regarding the company's products and services. Others might include a company history; a list of company officers; financial information, such as historical stock performance or financial statements; and employment information.

The Internet and commercial online services are also excellent sources for researching companies in periodicals. Today, most of the country's largest newspapers (including the *New York Times* and *Wall Street Journal*), as well as magazines, trade publications, and regional business periodicals, have gone online. You can simply type in the company name, and search the publication for references to that company. Many publications even allow you to search their archives going back several years (access may be restricted to subscribers).

The databases you choose to search will depend upon what information you are seeking. If you want to find a list of all financial consulting firms in Chicago, a database like the SuperPages is probably adequate. However, if you are preparing for a job interview as a high-level financial analyst, you might benefit from a service like Dun & Bradstreet.

You will often find that companies are listed in more than one database. You may be tempted to simply disregard the additional information and move on to the next company. However, it's wise to compare the information contained in the different databases. If the information is consistent, then it's probably safe to assume that it's correct; however, if the two sources conflict, you should try to find a third source to determine which information is accurate. It's also likely that many databases will contain different information; one may have financial information, and another may have a list of the chief executives. You should also be sure to watch the timeliness of the information you are finding; while most online databases are updated frequently, that is not always the case.

Researching Whenever and Wherever You Want

There are many advantages to researching companies online. The first is convenience; you can search right from your own home computer instead of going to the library or contacting an employment service firm. This convenience is especially valuable for last-minute job interviews. For instance, say you receive a call at three o'clock, asking you to come in for an interview the next morning. In the past, you might have panicked because you wouldn't have had adequate time for research. But, with the Internet, the information is right at your fingertips (as long as you know where to find it). Researching companies can go much faster when the information is only a few keystrokes away. You no longer have to carve out a large part of your day to go to the library and do research.

Where to Look

New resources for researching potential employers are popping up regularly on the World Wide Web. To find additional resources, you can tap into job hunting meta-lists, such as Purdue University's Center for Career Opportunities (**www.cco.purdue.edu/student/jobsitesn.html**), which provides links to numerous other career resources.

Listed below are several examples of Web sites that can be used to search for employers. These databases can be accessed free of charge, although there are several others that do charge small fees for searches.

CareerCity.com
www.careercity.com

If you've ever used one of the many *JobBank* books in your job search, you know how helpful their detailed information on the nation's top employers can be. CareerCity.com takes much of this information and makes it available online. All you need to do is type in your criteria and, if the company is part of the *JobBank* family of employers (tens of thousands of companies are), you will be presented with some of their vital statistics. The site also provides links to companies that have registered their Web sites. Even if your interview is with an employment agency rather than an actual employer, CareerCity.com provides links to thousands of American employment agencies with the same detailed information.

CompaniesOnline

www.companiesonline.com

Run by the Lycos Network, CompaniesOnline offers Webgoers information on more than 13,000 public and private companies. When you execute a search, the link will display such basic information as phone number, address, employee size, and annual sales. By clicking on the link, you will be allowed more in-depth information, including the big cheese's name and title, company DUNS number, SIC codes, and all of the company's Web addresses (this is a good way to find out about the company's parent or any subsidiaries that might exist).

Edgar Online

www.edgar-online.com

EDGAR (Electronic Data Gathering, Analysis, and Retrieval System) is the electronic filing arm of the Securities and Exchange Commission (SEC). All publicly traded companies are required by law to file certain documents with the SEC. Some international companies also file with EDGAR, but this is not mandatory. Job hunters can search the database for specific companies, and are likely to find such information as quarterly and annual reports.

Hoover's Online: The Business Network

www.hoovers.com

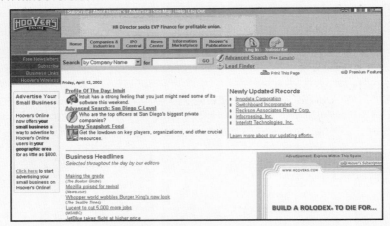

Geared toward the businessperson, Hoover's Online makes company information (general summary, key players, recent news headlines) available to you, the job seeker as well. The site is well organized and provides a variety of links, including links to current opportunities that exist at each company. While you're probably not interested in the positions they have available (if you have, after all, been called in for an interview), you may be interested in reading the listings to get a better sense of the type of employee they are looking for.

Jobfind.com

www.jobfind.com

Jobfind.com is profiled elsewhere in this book, and with good reason. In addition to providing tons of job postings, the site offers job seekers the chance to research these companies further. They offer several hundred company profiles with links to current openings.

Lexis-Nexis
www.lexis-nexis.com

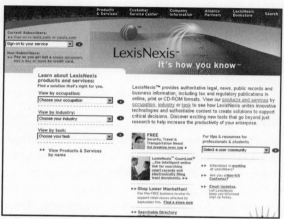

Lexis-Nexis offers a variety of services available in books, on CD-ROM, and on the Web. Overall, the Lexis-Nexis database offer access to three billion documents and thousands of individual databases. Well over a million subscribers conduct hundreds of thousands of searches on the service every day. The service offers information on industries and professions. NEXIS is the part of the service that is responsible for developing and selling business, financial, and public record information to businesses and the government. NEXIS is the largest online service of its type, and offers comprehensive industry and company reports.

My Job Search
www.myjobsearch.com
Here's another all-in-one site that can help you find a job, prepare for the interview, research a company, and negotiate a fair salary—all with one visit! This site is an invaluable source for job search information, no matter what phase of the game you are at. As much of the information is in the form of links to other sites, My Job Search can offer you access to a lot more information than your typical job site that tries to do it all on its own.

SuperPages

www.superpages.com

While not specifically designed for job hunters, SuperPages (formerly known as the Web's Big Book) contains the names, addresses, and phone numbers of hundreds of thousands of businesses throughout the country. You can search the extensive database by category, business name, state, and city. SuperPages can be tremendously useful for job interviews: By selecting a particular company in your targeted list, you'll see a detailed map of the area near the business, with the company's exact location highlighted (not available for all listings).

WetFeet.com

www.wetfeet.com

This completely comprehensive site will give you the lowdown on a particular career, industry, or company, all with the click of a mouse. The site will also allow you to type in your industry, ZIP code, and state and learn about what the average person in your position (or desired position) is making nowadays. The site offers specific advice to those who are just starting out, those who are changing careers, and student and MBAs. While the companies they offer research on are some of the bigger name companies within each industry, this can help you if you're looking to research the competition for a small start-up. Whether you're looking to get your feet wet or dive right in, WetFeet.com can answer just about any question you may want to ask.

Searching on Company Web Sites

As mentioned earlier, a company's home page on the World Wide Web is often one of the best sources of information for job hunters. You can learn the company's history and read their mission statement all in one place. Many sites for larger public companies include information for stockholders, like financial statements, annual reports, earnings reports, and stock quotes. Many Web sites also contain press releases where you can read about recent developments within the company (such as new product launches), changes among executives, or other important company news.

The tone of a home page can also be a good way to get a feel for the company's corporate culture. For instance, on Ben & Jerry's site **(www.benjerry.com)**, lighthearted animated cows and clouds are consistent with the laid-back, easy-going culture that the company promotes. Arthur Andersen's home page **(www.arthurandersen.com)**, on the other hand, has the professionalism and polish that is appropriate for an international accounting firm.

For many job hunters, the most valuable information to be found on a home page is employment information. Many of this country's leading employers, from Adobe Systems, Inc. **(www.adobe.com)** to Wal-Mart **(www.wal-mart.com)**, post job listings on their home pages. Home pages that don't contain job listings usually include some general information on how to apply for a job, such as a postal or e-mail address. Others go into a little more detail, outlining requirements for some common positions and describing the departments within the company. In either case, this is usually more information than you can get from most employer databases, or from speaking to a human resources representative within the company.

Looking at a company's Web page is like a one-stop shopping spree for job hunters. Instead of calling companies for annual reports, searching through executive directories for the name of the second vice-president of marketing, and poring over old business periodicals looking for news regarding a potential employer, you can visit the company's Web page and find this information. Some sites will have more information than you could possibly need, while others only skim the surface.

Unfortunately, looking up a company's URL is not as simple as finding a number in a phone book. Luckily, there are plenty of Web search engines and directories that can help you find the URLs of thousands of companies. **The Career Resource Center (www.careers.org)** is a good resource to start with. This meta-list of job hunting resources contains thousands of links to employers, job listings, reference materials, and more. You can either perform a broad search of all general Web directories, or browse through the more manageable category lists, such as technology companies or financial services.

Another great resource is **Qwest Dex** (formerly the Dot Com Directory) **(www.dotcomdirectory.com)**. This site is an exhaustive list of URLs that can be searched by company name, type, and location. The directory also includes information on financial reports, other Web addresses owned by the company, and general information on the company, including names of executives.

CHAPTER SEVEN

USENET NEWSGROUPS

Usenet newsgroups are one of the oldest and most misunderstood parts of the Internet. What was once the exclusive territory of this country's brain trust—academics, scientists, and top government officials—has developed into one of the most popular means of exchanging information on the Internet. At the same time, many new users are scared off by what they perceive as an intimidating Usenet culture. But by ignoring the discussion groups on Usenet, you could miss out on hundreds of potential job opportunities.

How Usenet Newsgroups Are Structured

Usenet is a collection of thousands of individual discussion groups, called newsgroups, which can be accessed through a direct Internet connection or through commercial online services like America Online or CompuServe. Anyone with access may post messages to these newsgroups, which are broadcast to interconnected computer systems. In some newsgroups, the message is sent to a "moderator" for approval before broadcast. The main purpose of the moderator is to ensure that advertising on newsgroups is kept to a bare minimum. Otherwise, messages are generally left uncensored. Usenet allows millions of users worldwide to discuss any topic imaginable—sports, current events, Elvis—you name it. Because newsgroups cover such a wide range of topics, they are broken down by hierarchies, or general categories, which enable you to find the topics you want more easily. Some of the main hierarchies are as follows:

- alt. (alternative)
- comp. (computers)
- humanities. (arts, literature, and other humanities)
- misc. (miscellaneous)
- news. (news for Usenet users)
- rec. (recreation)
- sci. (science)
- soc. (social issues)
- talk. (serious discussions about various issues)

There are also hundreds of local hierarchies, such as **atl.** (Atlanta), **il.** (Illinois), or **swnet.** (Sweden), which don't fall into any of the above hierarchies. The local hierarchies have newsgroups that cover subjects such as city politics, and some are online classifieds, with items like cars, bicycles, or kittens for sale.

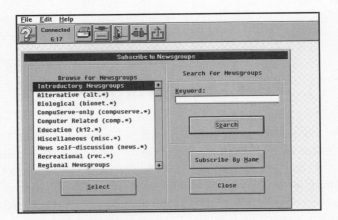

Newsgroups can be further broken down according to subject. For instance, **alt.backrubs** is in the alternative hierarchy under the subjects "backrubs." And they can get even more specialized: **alt.movies.hitchcock** and **alt.movies.monster** are in the alternative hierarchy, under the general subject "movies," discussing the movies of Alfred Hitchcock and the monster genre, respectively. Finally, each newsgroup contains discussion threads, which are basically a group of messages relating to the same topic. Every time someone posts a message regarding a new topic, a new thread is started.

It is this organizational and hierarchical structure that turns many people off to newsgroups. Many people open their newsreader to find a list of newsgroups, with directories and multiple subdirectories, and immediately close it because they are intimidated by what they see. They decide it's simply not worth it for them to figure out how the whole thing works, so they'll just stick with the Web. Unfortunately, they are missing out on one of the Internet's real gems.

Getting Started in Newsgroups

As mentioned earlier, Usenet newsgroups are accessible either through your Internet carrier or through commercial online services. Try **Keyword: Newsgroups** in AOL. If you have a regular Internet connection, you will need the help of a newsreader, such as Trumpet Newsreader, to actually read the messages in newsgroups. A newsreader simply organizes the thousands of available newsgroups, and allows you to read and post messages. Many Web browsers, like Netscape Navigator, have a built-in newsreader. Netscape's newsreader is called simply Netscape News. If you can't find a newsreader on your system, call your Internet provider and ask where to find one.

Once you're in Usenet, you should read the messages in the newsgroups **news.newusers.questions** and **news.announce.newusers**. In these newsgroups, you'll find answers to the most commonly asked question regarding Usenet, or you can post your own questions about Usenet. You can also find information such as a history of the Internet, rules for posting messages, and hints about the Usenet writing style.

After reviewing the basics of Usenet, post a test message to the newsgroups **alt.test** or **misc.test**. This test simply allows you to check to see that your newsreader is configured properly. If you cannot post test messages, ask your Internet carrier or commercial service provider for assistance.

If your test goes off without a hitch, then you are all set. Before you begin posting messages to dozens of newsgroups, there are a few basic facts about Usenet you need to know. First, different hierarchies and newsgroups have different tones to their discussions. In general, **alt.** newsgroups are more casual, while the **comp.** and **sci.** newsgroups are formal and factual. **Talk.** newsgroups discuss serious subjects in a serious manner. It's important to take the time to get a feel for a newsgroup; this can usually be done simply by reading a few days' worth of messages. Doing this should decrease your chances of posting an inappropriate message. Chapter Six discusses netiquette in greater detail.

Using Usenet to Find Jobs

Besides being an outlet for discussions, Usenet newsgroups are also one of the best sources on the Internet for job listings. Usenet has hundreds of newsgroups dedicated to job postings, each with as many as several thousand current job listings.

You can use job-related newsgroups to look for full- and part-time positions, as well as short-term, contract, freelance, or consulting work. In fact, there are a number of newsgroups dedicated specifically to postings for contractual labor. The majority of job-related newsgroups are local, but you can find plenty of national and industry-specific ones as well.

Instant Searches

Many job hunting Web sites, such as AllJobSearch.com **(www.alljobsearch.com)**, provide a search engine that allows you to simultaneously search employment newsgroups for job openings. Many search engines enable you to conduct searches on the World Wide Web or Usenet. Other sites, such as JobHunt **(www.jobhunt.org)**, do not list jobs, but do list job hunting resources, including Web sites and newsgroups. JobHunt is a good place to start for those interested in searching for specific newsgroups

Because so many newsgroups are targeted toward a specific region, they are an excellent resource for job hunters interested in relocating. If you're interested in moving to another city (or even another country), you can get a feel for the job market and send out your resume, without the cost of a subscription to an out-of-town newspaper.

Newsgroup job listings are also valuable because they contain more information than a traditional newspaper help-wanted advertisement. In general, these advertisements spell out the requirements and duties of the position in great detail. One big reason for this is cost—employers, employment agencies, and professional recruiters can post job listings free, regardless of how large or small the listing.

Major Job Posting Newsgroups

The newsgroups listed here are specifically for the posting of jobs, but you can often find one or two job postings in a newsgroup related to your profession, so you should try to check in fairly regularly with those types of groups. For instance, if you're a veterinarian, drop in on **alt.med.veterinary**, just in case something turns up.

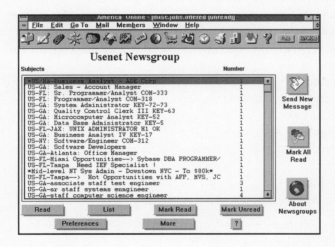

Beware of job postings that sound too good to be true. A number of sites will contain job postings with subjects along the lines of "$$MAKE MONEY AT HOME!$$." Usenet is one of the easiest places on the Web for anyone, regardless of morals, to access. It is not wise to believe that just because something is posted it's legitimate.

The following list is designed to help you find job openings in your particular region or field. It should also be noted that each individual

Internet service provider decides which newsgroups to carry; therefore, not all newsgroups will be available to everyone.

Newsgroups by Geographic Region

NORTHEAST/MID-ATLANTIC

balt.jobs
Employment opportunities in Baltimore, Maryland.

conn.jobs.offered
Employment opportunities in Connecticut.

ct.jobs
Employment opportunities in Connecticut.

dc.jobs
Employment opportunities in Washington, DC.

ithaca.jobs
Employment opportunities in the area of Ithaca, New York.

li.jobs
Employment opportunities on Long Island, New York.

md.jobs
Employment opportunities in Maryland and Washington, D.C.

me.jobs
Employment opportunities in Maine.

ne.jobs
Employment opportunities in New England.

ne.jobs.contract
Contract labor in New England.

nh.jobs
Employment opportunities in New Hampshire.

niagara.jobs
Employment opportunities in the Niagara region of New York.

nj.jobs
Employment opportunities in New Jersey.
nyc.jobs
Employment opportunities in New York City.

nyc.jobs.contract
Contract labor and consulting opportunities in New York City.

nyc.jobs.misc
Discussion of the New York City job market.

nyc.jobs.offered
Employment opportunities available in New York City.

nyc.jobs.wanted
Positions wanted in New York City.

ny.jobs
Employment opportunities in the state of New York.

pa.jobs.offered
Employment opportunities in Pennsylvania.

pgh.jobs.offered
Employment opportunities in Pittsburgh, Pennsylvania.

pgh.jobs.wanted
Positions wanted in Pittsburgh, Pennsylvania.

phl.jobs.offered
Employment opportunities in Philadelphia, Pennsylvania.

phl.jobs.wanted
Employment opportunities in Philadelphia, Pennsylvania.

SOUTHEAST

alabama.birmingham.jobs
Employment opportunities in Birmingham, Alabama.
alabama.jobs
Employment opportunities in Alabama.

alt.jobs.nw-arkansas
Employment opportunities in northwest Arkansas.

atl.jobs
Employment opportunities in Atlanta, Georgia.

atl.resumes
Resumes for positions in Atlanta, Georgia.

fl.jobs
Employment opportunities in Florida.

hsv.jobs
Employment opportunities in Huntsville, Alabama.

lou.lft.jobs
Employment opportunities in Lafayette, Louisiana.

memphis.employment
Employment opportunities in Memphis, Tennessee.

tnn.jobs
Employment opportunities in Tennessee.

triangle.jobs
Employment opportunities in Research Triangle Park, North Carolina.

us.sc.columbia.employment
Employment opportunities in Columbia, South Carolina.

va.jobs
Employment opportunities in Virginia.

MIDWEST

akr.jobs
Employment opportunities in Akron, Ohio.

chi.jobs
Employment opportunities in Chicago, Illinois.

chi.jobs.offered
Employment opportunities in Chicago, Illinois.

cle.jobs
Employment opportunities in Cleveland, Ohio.

cmh.jobs
Employment opportunities in Columbus, Ohio.

ia.jobs
Employment opportunities in Iowa.

il.jobs.misc
Discussion of the Illinois job market.

il.jobs.offered
Employment opportunities in Illinois.

il.jobs.resumes
Resumes for positions in Illinois.

in.jobs
Employment opportunities in Indianapolis, Indiana.

kc.jobs
Employment opportunities in Kansas City, Missouri.

mi.jobs
Employment opportunities in Michigan

milw.job
Employment opportunities in Milwaukee, Wisconsin.

milw.jobs
Employment opportunities in Milwaukee, Wisconsin.

mn.jobs
Employment opportunities in Minnesota.
nebr.jobs
Employment opportunities in Nebraska.

oh.jobs
Employment opportunities and positions wanted in Ohio.

stl.jobs
Employment opportunities in St. Louis, Missouri.

stl.jobs.resumes
Resumes for positions in St. Louis, Missouri.

WEST/SOUTHWEST

austin.jobs
Employment opportunities in Austin, Texas.

az.jobs
Employment opportunities in Arizona.

ba.jobs
Employment opportunities in the San Francisco Bay area.

ba.jobs.resumes
Resumes for positions in the San Francisco Bay area.

co.jobs
Employment opportunities in Colorado.

houston.jobs
Employment opportunities in Houston, Texas.

houston.jobs.offered
Employment opportunities in Houston, Texas.

houston.jobs.wanted
Positions wanted in Houston, Texas.

la.jobs
Employment opportunities in Los Angeles, California.

nevada.jobs
Employment opportunities in Nevada.
nm.jobs
Employment opportunities in New Mexico.

nv.jobs
Employment opportunities in Nevada.

pdaxs.jobs.computers
Computer-related opportunities in Portland, Oregon.

pdaxs.jobs.engineering
Engineering and technical opportunities in Portland, Oregon.

pdaxs.jobs.management
Management opportunities in Portland, Oregon.

pdaxs.jobs.retail
Retail opportunities in Portland, Oregon.

pdaxs.jobs.sales
Sales opportunities in Portland, Oregon.

sac.jobs
Employment opportunities in Sacramento, California.

sat.jobs
Employment opportunities in San Antonio, Texas.

sdnet.jobs
Employment opportunities in San Diego, California.

seattle.jobs
Employment opportunities in Seattle, Washington.

seattle.jobs.offered
Employment opportunities in Seattle, Washington.

seattle.jobs.wanted
Positions wanted in Seattle, Washington.

tx.jobs
Employment opportunities in Texas.
ut.jobs
Employment opportunities in Utah.

utah.jobs
Employment opportunities in Utah.

vegas.jobs
Employment opportunities in Las Vegas, Nevada.

wyo.jobs
Employment opportunities in Wyoming.

NATIONWIDE (U.S.)

alt.bestjobsusa
Employment opportunities in the United States.

alt.jobs.jobsearch
Discussion related to searching for employment.

misc.jobs.contract
Discussion of both short- and long-term contract labor.

misc.jobs.misc
General issues of employment and careers.

misc.jobs.offered
Employment opportunities available nationwide.

misc.jobs.offered.entry
Entry-level employment opportunities available nationwide.

misc.jobs.resumes
Resumes for positions wanted in the United States.

us.jobs
Employment opportunities in the United States.

us.jobs.contract
Contract labor and consulting opportunities in the United States.

us.jobs.misc
Employment opportunities in the United States.

us.jobs.offered
Employment opportunities in the United States.

us.jobs.resumes
Resumes for positions wanted in the United States.

INTERNATIONAL

ab.jobs
Employment opportunities in Alberta, Canada.

alt.jobs.overseas
Employment opportunities worldwide.

aus.ads.jobs
Employment opportunities in Australia.

bc.jobs
Employment opportunities in British Columbia, Canada.

bermuda.jobs.offered
Employment opportunities in Bermuda.

can.jobs
Employment opportunities in Canada.

eunet.jobs
Employment opportunities in Europe.

euro.jobs
Employment opportunities in Europe.

ie.jobs
Employment opportunities in Ireland.

iijnet.jobs
Employment opportunities in Israel.

kw.jobs
Employment opportunities in Kitchener-Waterloo, Canada.

ont.jobs
Employment opportunities in Ontario, Canada.

ott.jobs
Employment opportunities in Ottawa, Canada.

qc.jobs
Employment opportunities in Quebec, Canada.

swnet.jobs
Employment opportunities in Sweden.

tor.jobs
Employment opportunities in Toronto, Canada.

uk.jobs
Employment opportunities in the United Kingdom.

uk.jobs.wanted
Discussion about seeking employment in the United Kingdom.

za.ads.jobs
Employment opportunities in South Africa.

Newsgroups by Industry

BUSINESS SERVICES

misc.business.consulting
Discussion of the consulting business.

CONSTRUCTION/ELECTRICAL ENGINEERING

alt.building.jobs
Building and construction-related opportunities nationwide.

alt.engineering.electrical.jobs
Employment opportunities in the electrical engineering field.

COMMUNICATIONS

alt.journalism.moderated
Moderated discussion group for journalists.

misc.writing
A discussion group for writers of all types.

COMPUTERS

cit.jobs
Computer-related employment opportunities nationwide.

prg.jobs
Computer programming employment opportunities nationwide.

EDUCATION

k12.chat.teacher
Discussion group for teachers.

misc.education
General discussion of the educational systems.

GOVERNMENT

dod.jobs
Employment opportunities with the U.S. Department of Defense.

LEGAL

misc.legal
Discussion of the legal profession.

SCIENTIFIC/MEDICAL

alt.medical.sales.jobs.resumes
Medical sales employment opportunities nationwide.

bionet.jobs
Biological science employment opportunities nationwide.

bionet.women-in-bio
Discussion of issues relevant to women in the field of biology.

bionet.microbiology
Discussion of issues related to microbiology.

hepnet.jobs
Discussion of issues relating to high-energy nuclear physics.

sci.med
Discussion group for those interested in science and medicine.

sci.med.pharmacy
Discussion of the pharmaceutical field.

sci.research.careers
Discussion of careers relating to scientific research.

sci.research.postdoc
Employment opportunities in postdoctoral scientific research.

CHAPTER EIGHT

NETWORKING ONLINE

Ask anyone in the employment industry—consultants, outplacement specialists, HR professionals—and they will probably tell you that the best way to find a job is through networking. In fact, one common figure estimates that 80 percent of all jobs are found through networking. That said, establishing a solid, extensive network of contacts within your field of interest should be a top priority.

While some may think that top executives and industry insiders are the only people who benefit from networking, that is not the case. The development of specialized online discussion groups has made it easier for all job hunters to meet and interact with other professionals in the same field or industry. Every day, thousands of job hunters log on to the Internet's Usenet discussion groups or mailing lists, or visit the special interest groups (SIGs) on commercial online services in order to discuss issues and developments relevant to the field, compare experiences, or exchange information, including employment opportunities.

Usenet discussion groups, mailing lists, and SIGs are ideal for networking since they were designed so that people interested in the same things could discuss their similar interests by posting and reading messages. Today, there are hundreds of online discussion groups on virtually any topic, ranging from religion to politics to popular TV shows. The dozens of career-related discussion groups available cover fields like accounting, education, journalism, and microbiology.

The main objective of networking is to become visible to prospective employers. Other benefits of online networking include:

- **Discussion group participants often include human resources representatives and hiring managers**, who often lend their expertise by discussing the qualities they look for in employees. Many recruiters acknowledge visiting field-specific discussion groups to look for potential job candidates.

- **Participating in online discussion groups brings far greater exposure than going to a meeting of a local industry group.** A discussion group's audience is most often nationwide, and may include participants from around the world.
- **Monitoring discussion groups makes it easy to determine what skills and experiences employers are looking for.** For instance, do most of the other participants have their MBAs? It's also a good way to find out which companies are hiring, and what the hot topics and issues in the field are.

Job hunters should look at three main areas as potential networking resources: Usenet newsgroups, mailing lists, and special interest groups. These forums were designed expressly for the purpose of disseminating and receiving information. At the same time, keep an eye out for Web sites of industry organizations and associations. They can be a good way to keep up with the latest developments and advances in a particular field, and to keep abreast of the hot issues in that field.

The Importance of Netiquette

"Netiquette" is a combination of the words "network" and "etiquette." Originally used to describe the rules surrounding Usenet newsgroups, netiquette now refers to the widely accepted do's and don'ts for using any type of online discussion group. It is essential that new users, or "newbies," are familiar with the netiquette of a group before joining the discussion; otherwise, they might get "flamed" (criticized and ridiculed by established group members).

The easiest way to avoid getting flamed is to spend time observing and reading the group's posted messages before attempting to join the discussion. Each discussion group, especially those on Usenet, has a particular tone and rules. Simply "lurking" (reading messages, but not posting your own) in a particular group will give you a good sense of the group's personality. This is also a good way to ensure that a particular group will really fit your interests.

When you are ready to join in the discussion, don't simply post a general message along the lines of "Hi, I'm new here and just wanted to drop in and say hello!" Post a message that asks for specific advice, or introduces an original thought or comment to the discussion. A boring, generic posting with a header like "Help!" or "Hire me!" will be ignored at best, and will get you flamed at worst. If you do get flamed—something that happens to everyone every now and then—just ignore it.

Following are some other basic rules of netiquette, as well as some general guidelines to follow in professional discussion groups:

- **In all postings, write in full and complete sentences,** and be sure that all spelling, punctuation, grammar, and capitalization are correct.
- **Don't type messages in all capital letters;** THE ONLINE EQUIVALENT OF SHOUTING.
- **Don't use "emoticons"** such as J (happy face), or L (frown), or common abbreviations like BTW (By the Way) and IMHO (In My Humble Opinion) that are commonly used in recreational discussion groups. These types of cutesy shorthand are out of place in a professional discussion group.
- **Understand the appropriate times to post or e-mail a reply to a particular message.** Many new and experienced users alike are often unsure of when to direct an e-mail to the message's author and when a reply should be posted to the group. In general, post a reply if your message is something the group as a whole could appreciate and learn from, but use e-mail if your comment only concerns the author. This is important because no one wants to participate in a discussion that is little more than a dialogue between two or three people.
- **Finally, use common netiquette and professionalism.** Just because you can't see the person, don't forget that there is somebody on the other end of that message. Be as respectful and tolerant of other people's ideas as you would be in a face-to-face discussion.

Networking on Usenet Newsgroups

Newsgroups are a terrific place for networking, with discussion groups to suit almost every interest. Newsgroups also tend to have the harshest rules of netiquette, due in part to the fact that—since newsgroups are one of the oldest areas of the Internet—their participants are more technologically savvy than the online world as a whole. At the same time, their users are extremely knowledgeable, and helpful to those who have taken the time to learn the rules. Please see Chapter Seven for a list of Usenet newsgroups.

Be Patient and Persistent

Do not expect to be besieged with job offers and contact names simply because you logged on to a professional discussion group and posted a message full of intelligence and insight. Networking online is a slow process. Just as in real life, relationships do not form overnight, and it takes time to build up trusted contacts. In fact, it may be months before any job leads materialize. That's why we suggest continually maintaining a presence in appropriate discussion groups—even when you are happily employed—since the opportunity of a lifetime may turn up when it's least expected.

Networking with Mailing Lists

Mailing lists, also known as list-serves or e-mail discussion groups, are like a cousin to Usenet discussion groups. Like newsgroups, mailing lists allow users to post and read messages that contain threads of discussions on various topics. What sets mailing lists apart from newsgroups is that instead of users logging in to a specific group and posting and reading messages online, subscribers automatically receive new messages (and post messages to the group) via e-mail. Many users like mailing lists because they allow users to monitor discussion groups simply by checking their e-mail.

To subscribe to a mailing list, send an e-mail to the list's administrator. The list administrator makes sure that all messages are sent to subscribers. Like other discussion groups, each mailing list has its own rules and guidelines, so be sure to research the list carefully before taking an active role in any discussions.

There are tens of thousands of mailing lists available, covering subjects like arts, business, health, politics, and religion. To find the mailing lists that match your interests, consult the selection of online directories that follow. Each directory contains contact information, such as the system administrator's e-mail address, for over 50,000 mailing lists.

Liszt, The Mailing List Directory
www.listz.com

This directory claims to be the largest directory of mailing lists, and it just may be, with tens of thousands of lists available for searching. The site allows you to search by keywords.

Publicly Accessible Mailing Lists

www.neosoft.com/internet/paml

This list is searchable by name, subject, or keyword. It contains hundreds of different subject classifications. Check under "jobs" or "employment" for job-related mailing lists, but check out lists in your field as well. This list is also posted to the Usenet newsgroups **news.lists.misc** and **news.answers** around the end of each month.

Special Interest Groups (SIGs)

SIGs are generally found on commercial online services, such as America Online and CompuServe, but are commonly found on the Web as well. SIGs, like newsgroups, are a means by which people with similar interests can gather online to exchange ideas and information. While the groups are called different names on each service—forums, bulletin boards, roundtables—they are known collectively as SIGs.

SIGs differ from newsgroups in a number of ways: First, SIGs have smaller audiences, because fewer people subscribe to commercial online services than have access to the Internet. Also, most SIGs have moderators (called sysops, or system operators) who monitor the discussion to be sure that the comments are relevant to the specific group. They also make sure that the discussions don't get out of hand which can occasionally happen (this is usually called a "flame war"). And in most special interest groups, the main subject is subdivided into smaller directories, which make it easy to pinpoint the exact topic you want to discuss.

Networking Through Professional Organizations

Virtually every major professional organization maintains a Web page. These Web sites are an inexhaustible resource for jobseekers. Web pages enable organizations to lay out their information in a neat and user-friendly manner. The Web sites of professional organizations can include: listings for job openings nationwide; the location and dates of both major and minor events, including job fairs; general information on the relevant industry; and forums for discussing news and events with members. There is also often basic information on how to start or maintain a career in whichever industry or group the organization represents.

For every major (and some not so major) job category or industry, there is usually at least one professional organization that represents it.

The following is an alphabetical list of many of the major professional organizations.

Advertising Research Foundation
www.arfsite.org

Air Transport Association of America
www.air-transport.org

Air & Waste Management Association
www.awma.org

Alliance for Children and Families
www.alliancel.org

The Aluminum Association
www.aluminum.org

American Academy of Nurse Practitioners
www.aanp.org

American Accounting Association
www.aaa-edu.org

American Apparel Manufacturers
www.americanapparel.org

American Association for Higher Education
www.aahe.org

American Association of Advertising Agencies
www.aaaa.org

American Association of Engineering Societies
www.aaes.org

American Association of Healthcare Consultants
www.aahc.net

American Association of Pharmaceutical Scientists
www.aaps.org

American Astronautical Society
www.astronautical.org

American Bankers Association
www.aba.com

American Bar Association
www.abanet.org

American Bookseller Association
www.bookweb.org

American Design Drafting Association
www.adda.org

American Film Institute
www.afi.com

American Frozen Food Institute
www.affi.com

American Hospital Association
www.aha.org

American Institute of Architects
www.aia.org

American Institute of CPAs
www.aicpa.org

American Institute of Chemical Engineers
www.aiche.org

American Institute of Contractors
www.aicnet.org

American Iron and Steel Institute
www.steel.org

American Marketing Association
www.marketingpower.com

American Nuclear Society
www.ans.org

American Society for Clinical Laboratory Science
www.ascls.org

American Society of Civil Engineers
www.asce.org

American Society of Composers, Authors & Publishers
www.ascap.com

American Society of Landscape Architects
www.asla.org

American Society of Mechanical Engineers
www.asme.org

American Society of Travel Agents
www.astanet.com

American Textile Manufacturers
www.atmi.org

American Trucking Association
www.trucking.org

American Women in Radio & Television
www.awrt.org

Americans for the Arts
http://artsusa.org

Associated Builders & Contractors
www.abc.org

Association for Clinical Chemistry
www.aacc.org

Association for Computing Machinery
www.acm.org

Association for Manufacturing Excellence
www.asme.org

Association for Manufacturing Technology
www.mfgtech.org

Association of American Publishers
www.publishers.org

Association of Management Consulting Firms
www.amcf.org

Automotive Service Association
www.asashop.org

Biotechnology Industry Organization
www.bio.org

Catholic Charities USA
www.catholiccharities.org

The Center for Software Development
www.center.org

College & University Personnel Association
www.cupa.org

The Competitive Telecommunications Association
www.comptel.org

Electrochemical Society
www.electrochem.org

Electronic Publishing Association
www.epaonline.org

The Engineering Center
www.engineers.org

Equipment Leasing Association of America
www.elaonline.com

The Fashion Group International
www.fgi.org

HTML Writers Guild
www.hwg.org

Institute of Clean Air Companies
www.icac.com

Insurance Information Institute
www.iii.org

International Advertising Association
www.iaaglobal.org

International Association of Food Industry Suppliers
www.iafis.org

Internet Professional Publishers Association
www.ippa.org

Marketing Research Association
www.mra-net.org

Motor and Equipment Manufacturers Association
www.mema.org

National Aeronautic Association
www.naa-usa.org

National Association of Broadcasters
www.nab.org

National Association of Credit Management
www.nacm.org

National Association of Home Builders
www.nahb.com

National Association of Manufacturers
www.nam.org

National Association of Personnel Services
www.napsweb.org

National Association of Realtors
www.realtor.com

National Association of Social Workers
www.naswdc.org

National Association of Tax Practitioners
www.natptax.com

National Glass Association
www.glass.org

National Medical Association
www.nmanet.org

National Paralegal Association
www.nationalparalegal.org

National Recreation & Park Association
www.nrpa.org

National Restaurant Association
www.restaurant.org

National Retail Federation
www.nrf.com

National Society of Accountants
www.nsacct.org

National Society of Professional Engineers
www.nspe.org

Newspaper Association of America
www.naa.org

Printing Industries of America and the Graphic Arts Information Network
www.gain.org

Professional Aviation Maintenance Association
www.pama.org

Public Relations Society of America
www.prsa.org

Securities Industry Association
www.sia.com

Society for Information Management
www.simnet.org

Society for Mining, Metallurgy & Exploration
www.smenet.org

Technical Association of the Pulp & Paper Industry
www.tappi.org

CHAPTER NINE

COMPUTERIZED INTERVIEWS AND ASSESSMENT TESTS

Many companies, especially those that regularly hire large numbers of employees, are now having candidates complete a computerized job interview in place of an initial screening interview with a human resources representative. Like a traditional screening interview, the computer asks the candidate questions regarding their work history, background, skills, and qualifications, usually in true/false or multiple choice formats. Once the interview is complete, the computer provides the interviewer with a summary of the candidate's answers. Among other things, this summary might recommend bringing the candidate in for a face-to-face interview, and provide the interviewer with a list of follow-up questions for the second interview.

Candidates who have taken computer-assisted interviews give high marks to the computer; many report being less anxious. Human resources professionals like the system because it streamlines the hiring process and makes it more efficient. Companies that use computer-assisted job interviews report higher productivity, improved customer service, lower employee turnover and absenteeism, and less theft in the workplace.

Computerized job interviews are based on the principle of the structured job interview. Structured job interviews, which have long been valued by human resources professionals, are simply interviews where the same prescribed set of questions are asked of every candidate applying for positions within a company. Advocates to the structured interview say that it brings a consistency and fairness to the hiring process that is lacking when non-structured interviews are used.

The standardized format of the interview allows recruiters to more easily compare candidates' responses—each candidate gets asked the same questions in exactly the same way. Also, each question is carefully phrased so the interviewer doesn't have to worry about breaking any employment laws. Structured interviews also gather more information in less time than non-structured interviews.

Brooks Mitchell, Ph.D., founder and president of SHL Aspen Tree Software and a leader in the field of computer-assisted job interviews, was the first person to see how easily a computer could perform the initial screening interview. After all, he reasoned, what could be more consistent and impartial than a computer? Mitchell based his idea on the structured job interview and, in 1978, administered the first computer-assisted job interview in a large New Jersey plant. Since then, the use of computer-assisted interviews has continued to grow in fields and companies that traditionally hire large volumes of workers such as banks, hospitals, hotels, and retailers. These types of companies can have hundreds of entry-level job openings each year. Since the computer screens out any unqualified candidates, the hiring manager spends time only with those candidates who have the skills and qualifications necessary for the job.

What to Expect from a Computer-Assisted Job Interview

A computer-assisted job interview proceeds in much the same way as a traditional job interview: You get called for an interview, schedule a mutually convenient time to meet, come into the office, and meet with a human resources representative. However, instead of a face-to-face screening, you will be led to a computer workstation, where you will be given instructions on how to take the computer-assisted job interview. Most interview programs are intuitive and easy to navigate. You are generally given a time limit, usually about 30 minutes, in which to finish the interview.

Expect to be asked about one hundred questions regarding your educational background, employment history, job skills, and work ethic. Here is an example of some questions you might expect from the ApView computer-assisted interview from SHL Aspen Tree Software:

1. Are you currently employed?
   A. Yes
   B. No

2. Why did you leave your last job, or why do you want to leave your present job?
   A. I was dismissed
   B. I was laid off
   C. To take a better job
   D. Relocation
   E. To go to school
   F. I am not leaving my present job
   G. Other reason

3. How often do/did you experience conflict with your co-workers?
   Often
   Sometimes
   Rarely
   Never
   Cannot say

4. What kind of recommendation do you think your present or most recent supervisor would give you?
   Outstanding
   Above average
   Average
   Below average
   I don't know

5. At previous jobs, were you able to develop new or better ways of doing the work assigned to you?
   Most of the time
   Usually
   Sometimes
   Seldom
   Never

In the past, most computerized job interviews consisted entirely of multiple choice or true/false questions, but now some computerized interview systems contain a number of questions that require more extended, written responses. ApView, for example, offers its customer companies the option of using open-ended questions instead of, or in addition to, multiple-choice questions. Naturally, these types of answers are reviewed by a recruiter or hiring manager, not a computer. Most computer-assisted interviews are custom-made for each company or position. Generally, the interview is developed to address specific issues for a given position or family of positions. This eliminates the possibility that you will be asked questions that are irrelevant to the position for which you are applying.

You should answer the questions in a computer-assisted job interview just as you would in a traditional job interview. Don't exaggerate your skills and accomplishments. For instance, don't tell a computer you have five years' experience in retail if, in reality, you only have experience as a seasoned shopper. A computer-assisted interview is only the first step; if you get selected for a face-to-face interview, the interviewer will see from your application and resume that you were lying to the computer.

What's more, it's important to be more accurate with computerized interviews because, unlike their human counterparts, computers will immediately pick up on any inconsistencies in your responses. A human interviewer may be too distracted to pick up on any contradictions during an interview, but a computer is programmed to flag inconsistencies for the interviewer, resulting in your not being considered for a position or in several difficult follow-up questions in a second interview.

What the Computer Tells the Interviewer

Once you have completed the interview, the recruiter will explain to you the next steps in the interviewing process. Generally, the program will analyze your responses and present a summary to the recruiter. The recruiter will read the report and then decide whether you have the qualifications that would warrant a second interview. Among other things, the report summarizes basic background information, like education level and length of employment with your past or current company. It will also highlight those questions where you had an abnormally long pause before responding. This is done because several studies have shown that it takes longer for a person to tell a lie than it does to tell the truth. The report also flags inconsistencies and contradictions in your responses. Most programs will also provide the recruiter with a list of follow-up questions that should be asked in a second interview based on your answers to the computerized interview. For instance, in the sample questions listed earlier, the follow-up to question number five is, "Give me an example of something you developed on a previous job that enhanced a work assignment."

Some programs will also compare the results of your interview with a standardized employee profile that has been developed for a particular company. By comparing your answers with those of successful hires, the computer can predict—usually with measurable success—whether or not you will be a good employee.

It's Just One More Tool

Even after the most advanced and detailed computer-assisted job interview, a computer will never make the final hiring decision. It simply presents a report to an individual recruiter, and it is up to this individual to analyze the data provided and determine whether or not to invite a candidate in for a second interview. So don't worry about your fate being in the hands of a machine; for better or worse, the final decision is still left up to a real person.

Why Employers Like Computer-Assisted Job Interviews

SHL Aspen Tree Software, the makers of the ApView interview system, reports that employers like computer-assisted job interviews because they ensure that each candidate is thoroughly and impartially screened. With computer-assisted interviews, the information gathered is more accurate and reliable. What's more, advocates of these systems believe that the selectivity of the computer screens out borderline candidates who may have otherwise advanced, thus improving the overall quality of employees. One company reported a 33 percent lower turnover rate in the first six months of using a computer-assisted interview for the initial screening interview. Some other advantages of the computer-assisted job interview include:

- Avoids traditional interviewing problems, such as forgetting to ask important questions or letting personal feelings interfere with the interview.
- Gathers more information about a candidate in one-third the time it would take a human interviewer.
- Information is more accurate—applicants are more likely to be honest with a computer.

Companies also often use computerized interviews for situations where accuracy and honesty are essential, such as exit interviews, in-house promotion interviews, or to measure employee morale and attitude. Since people are generally more honest with a computer, companies can get a more accurate reading of their employees.

The Internet Job Interview

This method of interviewing is quickly gaining popularity, especially for long-distance job hunting. For instance, say you're applying for a position with a company in Chicago, but you live in San Francisco. If you are hooked up online, you can simply complete a screening interview on your own home computer—instead of paying for an expensive flight and hotel room. Again, the process starts like any other: You are contacted for an initial screening interview, but instead of scheduling an initial telephone or face-to-face interview, you are provided with a password that gives you access to the company's in-house computer system. Once you log on, the process is essentially like that of a computer-assisted job interview. You are asked basic questions about your background and work experience, and the computer generates a report for the recruiter. Again, companies like this method because it's a big time-saver, but it is also beneficial to job hunters, since travel expenses for job interviews are usually paid for only the most high-level executives or most sought-after college recruits.

Computerized Assessment Tests

Assessment tests are nothing new to the world of job hunting. For years, job applicants have been asked to take all kinds of tests to evaluate their suitability for a job. The reasoning behind these tests is simple: Hiring new employees is time-consuming and expensive. By carefully screening applicants with both structured, computer-assisted job interviews and computerized assessment tests, recruiters can greatly reduce the chances that a new hire will leave only after only a few short months, and consequently, the time and expense of another candidate search will be avoided.

Employers generally use three main types of assessment tests: **skills**, **integrity**, and **personality**. The purposes of each of these tests are pretty basic: Skills tests determine if you have the ability to do a particular job; integrity tests help determine whether you will be a trustworthy employee; and personality tests tell the interviewer if your disposition is suited to a particular position. Depending upon the nature of the position you are applying for, you may be asked to take one, two, or all three of these tests. Most positions require some type of skills test, for example, a math test for accountants or a typing test for administrative assistants. Some computer programmers are even asked to write a short program as part of their pre-employment testing. If you are applying for a position where you'll be dealing with goods or money, you will probably be required to take an integrity test. Personality or psychological tests can be used in virtually any situation, but are especially common if you are interviewing for a management position or one where you would be working with sensitive materials.

Pinkerton, the well-known security and investigation firm, stresses that prevention—by using pre-employment screening such as personality and integrity testing—is the best way to reduce or eliminate serious workplace issues such as theft, drug use, or even employee violence. To this end, Pinkerton has created a number of automated integrity, personality, and skills tests including the Stanton Profile, the Stanton Survey, and the Adult Personality Survey.

Taking a Computerized Assessment Test

Computerized assessment tests are generally administered after the initial screening interview, while skills tests can often be part of the initial screening process. However, personality and integrity tests are usually given as one of the last steps of the interviewing process. If you are asked to take a computerized assessment test, your interviewer will likely lead you to a semi-private or private room with a computer. After you receive instruction on how to use the program, the test will be administered, usually within a specified time limit. Depending on the nature of the test, you may simply answer multiple choice or true/false questions, or you may transcribe written information into a specific computer program. Integrity and personality tests typically contain upwards of 100 questions. Most are of the multiple choice, yes/no, true/false, always/some-times/never variety. When your time is up, the computer will score your work, and, if applicable, compare your answers to a specified profile. The computer then generates a report for the interviewer to review. It should be made clear that the computer doesn't actually tell the employer whether someone should or should not be hired; it simply tells the recruiter how a candidate fits in relation to other candidates.

Computerized Skills Tests

Skills tests are the most straightforward types of computerized assessment tests. These tests simply determine your proficiency in various word processing, spreadsheet, and database programs. With these computerized programs, you are asked to do some basic exercises using the various applications, and you are tested on your accuracy. Employment agencies often employ these types of tests to determine a job seeker's skill level before placing them with a company.

Computerized skills tests cover all fields: An accountant or engineer may be tested on their mathematical or logical reasoning skills; a computer programmer might need to write a few lines of code or debug a problematic program. You may even be asked to take a test that measures reaction time, or that tests your memory.

Computerized skills tests are measured on your raw score. Your score is then measured against a mean, or average score of everyone who has taken the test. For example, if you score a 75, and the mean is 68, that will show the employer that you have above-average skills. Unfortunately, there's no real way to prepare for skills tests. The best you can do is prepare for the type of test, such as a typing or math test, that is likely to be administered during a job interview by brushing up on those skills.

Computerized Integrity Tests

Integrity tests, such as Pinkerton's Stanton Profile, are another type of computerized assessment test. Basically, these tests measure your honesty and morals. The Stanton Survey is designed to measure the moral standard by which you live. This doesn't mean an employer is trying to find out whether you have the capacity to embezzle company funds or steal from the cash register; an applicant's level of honesty and moral standard can also help determine whether someone is likely to be tardy, socialize excessively during work hours, leave early, take long lunches, "borrow" office equipment, and so forth.

Integrity tests allow employers to measure the reliability, work ethic, and trustworthiness of a candidate. These traits are all important indicators of a candidate's future performance. For instance, a recruiter might question the candidacy of an applicant who, on his integrity test, stated that it's all right to steal sometimes.

When taking an integrity test, try to avoid absolutes likely always or never. No one is likely to believe you if you say you have "never" in your whole life lied, or you have "never" gotten so much as a parking ticket. Be honest, but don't reveal more than you have to.

Computerized Personality Tests

Personality tests are the most complex of all computerized assessment tests. These are generally used to test a candidate's personal make-up to see if his or her personality is suited to a particular job. Tests such as Pinkerton's Adult Personality Survey measure specific personality traits such as work motivation, adaptability, and trustworthiness. The results of a personality test are then compared against a standard, or norm, group that has been developed from all who have previously taken the test. For instance, if you are applying for a position as an insurance underwriter, your scores will be measured against a norm group of successful underwriters.

Companies like personality tests because they allow companies to see if you will "fit in" with the company and the positions, which is beneficial to both you and the employer. If you take a job only to realize, one month later, that you are not happy, the company has wasted time and money to train you while you have wasted time in a job that ultimately was not right for you. Another Pinkerton test is the Stanton Profile, a hybrid personality/skills test that measures general employability. This test measures your work preferences; your score is measured against the minimum requirements of a particular job. For instance, the test will ask you a question regarding your adaptability, a good trait for someone applying for a position as an administrative assistant, but not for someone working in a stock room, since that person will likely be doing the same tasks day after day with little variation.

While preparing for skills and integrity tests is difficult, preparing for personality tests is nearly impossible. First of all, many people aren't sure if they should let their "true" selves answer questions, or if they should answer questions based on the kind of personality they think the company is looking for. Experts differ on the subject. Some suggest you use your work personality, while others say you should just be yourself. Still others suggest coming up with a "character" based on successful friends and colleagues.

We suggest you look at what's helped you get where you are, and also what has held you back. If you have spent any time in the work force, you should realize that your work personality differs from your personality outside of work. Therefore, it is best to use what you have learned in the workplace. If you are new to the workplace, this logic still applies. Look at what traits and strengths have worked for you and brought success in the past, and focus on those.

As with the integrity tests, try to avoid using absolutes like "always" and "never" when taking personality tests. A large number of always and never answers might make it look like you are lying, or worse, be a signal of extreme behavior.

GLOSSARY
OF TERMS

Access: The ability to connect to a service or resource and receive information.

ActiveX Control: An add-on program that enhances the capabilities of an Internet Explorer browser; similar to a plug-in.

Address: The combination of letters and/or numbers that enables you to reach another computer or user online. People with online/Internet accounts have e-mail addresses where they receive their e-mail. A fictional example of an address is **yourname@computer.com**. On the Internet, the address of a Web site is also called a URL.

ADSL: An acronym for Asymmetric Digital Subscriber Line; a quicker way of using the non-voice part of a telephone line to send data; also known as DSL.

Agent: A software program that searches out information and brings it back to your computer.

American Standard Code for Information Exchange: *See ASCII.*

Archie: A software program that allows you to find files on an anonymous FTP site.

ARPANET: An acronym for Advance Research Projects Agency Network; the first computer network developed by the United States Department of Defense; the original ancestor of the Internet.

ASCII: An abbreviation for American Standard Code for Information Interchange, pronounced "ass-key." It is the most basic code for written documents (such as resumes or letters) that all computers understand. ASCII files contain no special formatting like italics or boldface. It was invented to enable different types of computers to communicate with each other. It's often referred to as DOS text or plain text.

Attachment: A file consisting of text, pictures, sound, or video that is sent with an e-mail message.

BPS: Stands for bits per second; it is the measurement of how quickly a modem can send and receive information. The slower your bps, the longer it takes to receive information.

Backbone: The central line or series of connections that forms the main pathway in a network; the backbone connects all the networks together.

Bandwidth: The amount of information you can actually send through a connection; bandwidth is usually measured in bits per second (BPS).

Baud: The scientific unit of measurement of data transmission speed. Usually measured as one bit per second. Not to be confused with BPS, which is the correct term for measuring modem speeds.

Binary File: A non-ASCII, non-text file.

BinHex: A method used to convert binary files (non-ASCII, non-text) into an ASCII format.

Bit: Short for binary digit; a bit is the smallest measurement of data; measuring the speed at which data is transmitted is often measured by bits per second (bps).

Bookmark: To store a site's Web page address, thereby eliminating the need to type in a URL every time you want to return to a particular site. This feature is found on most Web browsers.

Browser: A software program that locates Internet resources and displays them to users.

Bulletin Board System: Commonly abbreviated as BBS, a Bulletin Board System is like a mini-online service, catering to communities or to particular interests. Basically, it's a computer set up with communications software, a modem, and one or more phone lines. It's an easy way for users to meet, exchange information, and find computer files and software. Many BBSs also offer their users some form of Internet access.

Byte: A measurement of eight bits of computerized data.

Cache: The area of a computer's hard drive that stores the most recently accessed Web pages.

Chat: Sending messages back and forth in real time; messages appear instantly, as they are written.

Click: To press on the mouse button and cause another action to occur.

Clients: Special programs that retrieve information from other computers and computer networks called "servers."

Commercial Online Service: A company selling Internet access, usually offering a variety of other services as well, such as e-mail, chat rooms, news and information, and shopping.

Communications Software: A software program that enables you to use your modem; communications software controls the exchange of information between your modem and a remote modem.

Computer-Assisted Job Interview: A job interview conducted by a computer; the test usually consists of a series of True/False and multiple choice questions.

Computerized Assessment Tests: Tests administered by a computer that help determine job fit; tests usually fall into one of the following categories: Skills, Personality, and Integrity.

Configure: Adjusting the software settings so that a computer can connect to the Internet using an ISP.

Cookie: Information that a Web page automatically stores on your hard drive once you've viewed it; cookies will help a Web site recognize you when you visit again.

Cyberspace: A general term often used to refer to the nonexistent space that the Internet and all its functions inhabit; the term originated in William Gibson's 1984 novel *Neuromancer*.

Database: A large, organized collection of information that's stored electronically. A database's carefully constructed design enables users to search for and locate specific information—such as job listings in a particular field or location—quickly and easily.

Discussion Group: An electronic meeting place for people with shared interests to chat, discuss ideas and issues, and exchange information through the posting and reading of messages. It's the general term used when referring to Usenet newsgroups, mailing lists, or special interest groups on commercial online services.

Domain Name: An Internet site's registered name; the end of the domain name (.com, .edu, etc.) is the top-level domain that alerts you to what kind of site it is; the beginning of the domain name is the second-level domain, it is usually the name of the company or organization.

Download: To transfer data (such as files) from another computer to your own.

DSL: An acronym for Digital Subscriber Line; a quicker way of using the non-voice part of the telephone line to send data; also known as an ADSL.

Electronic Resume: A traditional resume that has been stripped of most of its formatting so that it can be easily read and searched by a computer.

E-mail: E-mail, or electronic mail, is a standard service that comes with most communications software, Internet connections, and commercial online services. It allows you to send and receive messages through your computer.

E-mail Discussion Group: A type of discussion group found on the Internet; also referred to as "mailing list" or "list serve."

Emoticons: Punctuation used to symbolize emotions; emoticons are often used in e-mail and newsgroups.

Encryption: The jumbling of messages and/or information so that they cannot be read without a decoding device.

Ethernet: One of the most common ways to network the computers in a LAN; can handle about 10 million BPS.

FAQ: Frequently Asked Questions. Compilation of questions (along with their answers) that are most commonly asked. Posted by most newsgroups, mailing lists, special interest groups, and other online services for the benefit of new or inexperienced users.

Filtering: Censoring questionable material by blocking access to it on the Internet, in newsgroups, or via e-mail. Parents often filter adult material so that their children are not exposed to it, and companies filter to monitor their employees.

Filtering Software: The software used in filtering.

Finger: A program that allows you to retrieve information about a user simply by typing in their e-mail address; while fingers normally only retrieve non-personal information, many Web sites do not allow incoming finger requests.

Flame: An angry or hostile e-mail message or newsgroup posting.

Flame war: The result of various angry or hostile messages being sent back and forth in an online discussion group.

Forum: A specific name for special interest groups or discussion groups found on various commercial online services and Web sites where participants can post and read messages regarding specific topics.

Frame: An independent part of a Web page; not all browsers are able to display frames.

Freeware: Public domain software files that are available to users free of charge.

FTP: An acronym for File Transfer Protocol; allows you to access and retrieve or send information over the Internet that is housed in a certain Web site; used in both private and public domains.

GIF: Acronym for Graphics Interchange Format; a file format that is often used to display images on the Web.

Gigabyte: A measurement one thousand times larger than a megabyte.

Gopher: Often referred to as the grandparent technology of the Web, Gopher is a menu-based system that easily allows users to explore all areas of the Internet, usually with the help of Gopher's search engines.

Graphical Browser: A browser that allows users to use a mouse instead of the keypad.

Hit: A term that is most often used on the World Wide Web; when a Web site claims to have had one million hits, the are essentially saying that one million people have visited their Web site.

Home Page: Home pages are maintained by companies, organizations, the government, educational institutions, and individuals. The home page is also referred to as the first page of a Web site, where you can find, for example, the main menu of options.

Host: A computer that provides some sort of service(s) to other computers in a network; functions could include access to particular files or access to the Internet.

HTML: Hypertext Markup Language, the text formatting language that makes use of hypertext and is used to write documents on the World Wide Web.

HTTP: Acronym for Hypertext Transfer Protocol; the command that moves hypertext pages over the Internet; any Web address begins with *http://*.

Hypertext: Hypertext enables users to jump from one page to another to access information, such as text, graphics, or music, through predefined links. It's the concept upon which the World Wide Web is based.

Icon: A picture that will execute a command when you click on it.

Intelligent Agent: A software program that locates information and understands context.

Interface: The onscreen look of the page that allows users to interact with their computers.

Internet: The global network of computers that transmits information via telephone lines, enabling computers from all over the world to communicate with each other. It's used by many different organizations, such as educational, commercial, and government institutions, to convey news, entertainment, and other information to users worldwide. It's also the general term used when referring to Gopher, Telnet, Usenet, and the World Wide Web.

Internet Explorer: A Web browser made by Microsoft.

Internet Relay Chat: A system allowing for real-time communication; often referred to as IRC.

Internet Service Provider: A company selling dial-up access to the Internet; also known as ISP.

Intranet: A sort of personalized internet system; intranets are found in companies so that information can be exchanged by co-workers, but is not available for public viewing.

ISDN: An acronym for Integrated Services Digital Network; a quicker way to move data over a telephone line; both ends are digital, not analog.

ISP: *See Internet Service Provider.*

JPEG: An acronym for Joint Photographic Experts Group; a file format that is often used to display images on the Web.

Jughead: The smaller of Gopher's two main search engines. Veronica is the other search engine.

Keyword: A word or short phrase that is used to search a database of documents or files. When filed, documents, such as resumes, are indexed using a particular set of words that refer to key concepts within that document. When you perform a keyword search, the computer searches all documents and files within a particular database (or databases) for matches between the keyword and one of the indexed words.

Kilobytes: A measurement equal to one thousand bytes of data.

Link: Created using hypertext, links are what connect you to a different site on the World Wide Web. The new connection may be with a different Web page or simply a file or subdirectory within a large site or down the same page. Links are most often represented by underlined words, though some may be presented as graphics.

List Serve: A type of discussion group found on the Internet; also referred to as "mailing list" or "e-mail discussion group."

Local Area Network: Also referred to as a LAN; one of the basic kinds of networks; in a LAN, computers are usually within a close physical proximity of one another, like in an office.

Log In: Often "log on." To connect with a remote computer or computer network, such as a commercial online service or BBS.

Lynx: A text-only browser; many UNIX-based operating systems use Lynx.

MacTP: The software a Macintosh computer needs to use the Internet; similar to the TCP/IP a PC needs to connect.

Mailing List: Also known as a list serve. A type of discussion group found on the Internet, in which users send and receive messages through e-mail.

Megabyte: A measurement of one million bytes; equal to one thousand kilobytes.

Meta-List: A "list of lists" found on the World Wide Web with links to Web sites and other Internet resources on a particular subject, such as job hunting. These lists are good time-savers since they generally include a short description or review of the site or service, so you won't waste time visiting irrelevant or low-quality sites. Plus, to access a particular site, you only need to click on the site name.

Modem: From Modulator/Demodulator. A communication device that converts data from computers into sound that is transmittable via a telephone line, thereby allowing remote computers to communicate with each other through ordinary phone lines. Information is now being transferred more and more via cable lines.

Moderator: The person who monitors a discussion group or special interest group on the Internet and ensures that information being posted is relevant to the topic at hand.

Mosaic: The first graphical browser and precursor to Netscape; it allowed users to point and click a mouse to navigate the Web.

MPEG: An acronym for Motion Pictures Experts Group; a file format that is often used to view video clips on the Internet.

Multimedia: The joint use of several different forms of media, such as text, sound, graphics, and video in a single application, such as a Web page or CD-ROM.

Netiquette: The established set of manners used when participating in Usenet newsgroups and other online discussion groups. It's important to be familiar with the netiquette of a particular newsgroup before jumping into the discussion. Created from combining the words "network "(or "Internet") and "etiquette."

Netizen: An Internet user who displays proper netiquette.

Netscape Communicator: A software package that includes the Netscape Navigator browser, an e-mail and newsreader program, tools for building a home page, and other features.

Network: Computers that are physically connected, usually through hardware, to facilitate the sharing of information. There are two basic kinds of networks: Local Area Networks (LANs), which are relatively close together, in the same office, for instance; and Wide Area Networks (WANs) in which the computers are scattered across cities, states, or countries. Technically, the Internet is considered a Wide Area Network.

Newbie: Internet slang for someone who is new to the Internet and the World Wide Web or to a particular newsgroup or discussion group.

Newsgroup: The name of online discussion groups found in Usenet. These electronic message boards are the most popular type of discussion group.

Newsreader: A software program that allows you to read and post messages to newsgroups.

Online: To be linked via modem to another computer or computer network. To say that you're "online" generally means that you are connected to the Internet.

Page: A document with text, pictures, or sound. Pages can be found on the World Wide Web.

Password: A secret word; passwords can allow you access to your computer, the Internet, a particular Web page, etc.

PGP: An acronym for Pretty Good Privacy; a software program that jumbles the text of an e-mail to protect one's privacy.

Plug-ins: Used to enhance the ability of your browser by allowing you to hear sounds, experience virtual reality, etc.; plug-ins are purchased as software.

POP: An acronym for Point of Presence; the location that an Internet service provider can connect to with a local telephone call.

Post: Post, or posting, is used as both a noun and verb. As a noun, a post is what you may find and read online, such as job listings or a message in a newsgroup. As a verb, post is when you send a messages or a document (like a resume) to a BBS, newsgroup, special interest group, or Web site.

PPP: An acronym for Point-to-Point Protocol; an account with an Internet service provider.

Protocol: The set of rules that determine how different computers exchange information. For instance, the documents in the Web address **http://www.yahoo.com** must be retrieved using hypertext ("http" stands for hypertext transfer protocol).

Pull-down Menu: A list of several choices that drops down when you click on it.

Push Technology: A system that sends customized information directly to a computer because of a user's previously state preference.

QuickTime: A file format that is often used to show short video clips on the Internet; developed by Apple Computer.

Search Engine: An information or database retrieval tool that enables users to quickly and easily search the vast amounts of information found on the World Wide Web (many also search Usenet).

Server: A main computer or computer network that relays information when "asked" by special software called "clients."

SET: An acronym for Secure Electronic Transaction; a standard used by credit card companies and online retail sites that jumbles information, making online shopping a safe transaction.

Shareware: Software files that are available free to users for a limited time only, called and "evaluation" period. After the evaluation period, you must pay in order to use the software.

SIG: *See Special Interest Group*

Site: A specific place on a commercial online service or the Internet (including the World Wide Web) where users can find information.

SLIT: An acronym for Single Line Internet Protocol; an account with an Internet service provider; an older version of a PPP.
Spam: Junk or excessive e-mail or messages.

Special Interest Group: The type of discussion groups found on commercial online services and Web site. Includes bulletin boards and forums.

SSL: An acronym for Secure Socket Layer; a system that jumbles information to protect one's privacy, it is often used by retail Web sites to ensure safe shopping.

Status Indicator: An icon that appears on your browser to indicate whether or not the browser is active.

TCP/IP: Acronym for Transmission Control Protocol/Internet Protocol; the set of rules that computer abide on the Internet to communicate with one another.

Tags: Codes employed in HTML that are used to execute certain functions; tags can be used to create links, or employ boldfaced or italicized print.

Telephony: A technology that allows for voice communication over the Internet; telephony may involve using microphones or computers, not telephones.

Telnet: A way of connecting to a remote computer or network over the Internet. You navigate Telnet by using command line prompts. It's also a type of Internet site that you may connect to. For example, you can Telnet directly to a Telnet site, or Telnet to a Gopher server.

Thread: A string of related messages on the same topic found in Usenet newsgroups and other discussion groups. It contains both original posts and replies to those posts.

Toolbar: A horizontal row of icons and verbal commands; each button will execute a different command.

UNIX: An operating system for computers; invented before Windows, UNIX was used heavily in the past and is still used today.

Upload: To transfer data (such as files) from your own computer to another computer.

URL: Short for Uniform Resource Locator. It's the uniquely identifiable address for any Web site—such as a file, directory, or other computer— on the World Wide Web. For instance, **www.whitehouse.gov** is the URL for the office of the President of the United States.

Usenet: Abbreviation of User's Network. This is a vast, international network of more than 20,000 different online discussion groups on practically every topic imaginable. Usenet is only one part of the Internet, and was created specifically to allow users to exchange news and other information.

Veronica: The larger of Gopher's two search engines; Jughead is the other search engine.

Virtual: Something that is close to being real; for example, the term "virtual reality" refers to a computer-generated program that feels like it is real, though it is not.

Virus: A computer program that runs unexpectedly on a computer; depending on the severity of the virus, these programs can impair your computer's ability to perform normal tasks interminably or even wipe out all your pre-existing programs.

Web Browser: Software, such as Netscape Navigator, that enables users to navigate the World Wide Web. It "reads" the hypertext documents on the Web, including text, intricate layouts, and graphics, and presents the information to the end users.

Web site: A group of pictures that are linked together because they belong to the same individual, company, institution or organization.

Wide Area Network: Also referred to as a WAN; one of the basic kinds of networks; in a WAN, computers are often scattered across several cities, states, or even countries; the Internet would be considered a Wide Area Network.

World Wide Web: A part of the Internet that uses hypertext links and graphics to convey all kinds of information—news, entertainment, and more. Hypertext links enable users to jump between different documents and files, making the Internet both simple and fun. Commonly referred to as the Web.

WYSIWYG: An acronym for "What You See Is What You Get"; a Web authoring tool that allows you to preview what a Web page will look like before you finish crating it; pronounced "wizzy wig."

INDEX

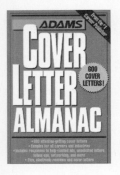

Adams Cover Letter Almanac

The *Adams Cover Letter Almanac* is the most detailed cover letter resource in print, containing 600 cover letters used by real people to win real jobs. It features complete information on all types of letters, including networking, "cold," broadcast, and follow-up. In addition to advice on how to avoid fatal cover letter mistakes, the book includes strategies for people changing careers, relocating, recovering from layoff, and more. $5^{1}/_{2}$" x $8^{1}/_{2}$", 738 pages, paperback, $12.95. ISBN: 1-55850-497-4.

Adams Cover Letter Almanac & Disk

Writing cover letters has never been easier! *FastLetter*™ software includes: a choice of dynamic opening sentences, effective following paragraphs, and sure-fire closings; a complete word processing program so you can customize your letter in any way you choose; and a tutorial that shows you how to make your cover letter terrific. Windows compatible. $5^{1}/_{2}$" x $8^{1}/_{2}$", 738 pages, *FastLetter*™ software included (one $3^{1}/_{2}$" disk), trade paperback, $19.95. ISBN: 1-55850-619-5.

Adams Resume Almanac

This almanac features detailed information on resume development and layout, a review of the pros and cons of various formats, an exhaustive look at the strategies that will definitely get a resume noticed, and 600 sample resumes in dozens of career categories. *Adams Resume Almanac* is the most comprehensive, thoroughly researched resume guide ever published. $5^{1}/_{2}$" x $8^{1}/_{2}$", 770 pages, paperback, $12.95. ISBN: 1-55850-358-7.

Adams Resume Almanac and Disk

Create a powerful resume in minutes! *FastResume*™ software includes: a full range of resume styles and formats; ready-to-use action phrases that highlight your skills and experience; a tutorial that shows you how to make any resume terrific; and a full word processor with ready-made layout styles. Windows compatible. $5^{1}/_{2}$" x $8^{1}/_{2}$", 770 pages, *FastResume*™ software included (one $3^{1}/_{2}$" disk), trade paperback, $19.95. ISBN: 1-55850-618-7.